Contents

ISBN: 978 1 80282 907 5
Editor: Paul Lunn
Senior editor, specials: Roger Mortimer
Email: roger.mortimer@keypublishing.com
Cover Design: Steve Donovan
Design: SJmagic DESIGN SERVICES, India
Advertising Sales Manager: Brodie Baxter
Email: brodie.baxter@keypublishing.com
Tel: 01780 755131
Advertising Production: Becky Antoniades
Email: Rebecca.antoniades@keypublishing.com

SUBSCRIPTION/MAIL ORDER
Key Publishing Ltd, PO Box 300, Stamford, Lincs, PE9 1NA
Tel: 01780 480404
Subscriptions email: subs@keypublishing.com
Mail Order email: orders@keypublishing.com
Website: www.keypublishing.com/shop

PUBLISHING
Group CEO and Publisher: Adrian Cox

Published by
Key Publishing Ltd, PO Box 100, Stamford, Lincs, PE9 1XQ
Tel: 01780 755131
Website: www.keypublishing.com

PRINTING
Precision Colour Printing Ltd, Haldane, Halesfield 1, Telford, Shropshire. TF7 4QQ

DISTRIBUTION
Seymour Distribution Ltd, 2 Poultry Avenue, London EC1A 9PU

Enquiries Line: 02074 294000.

Introduction

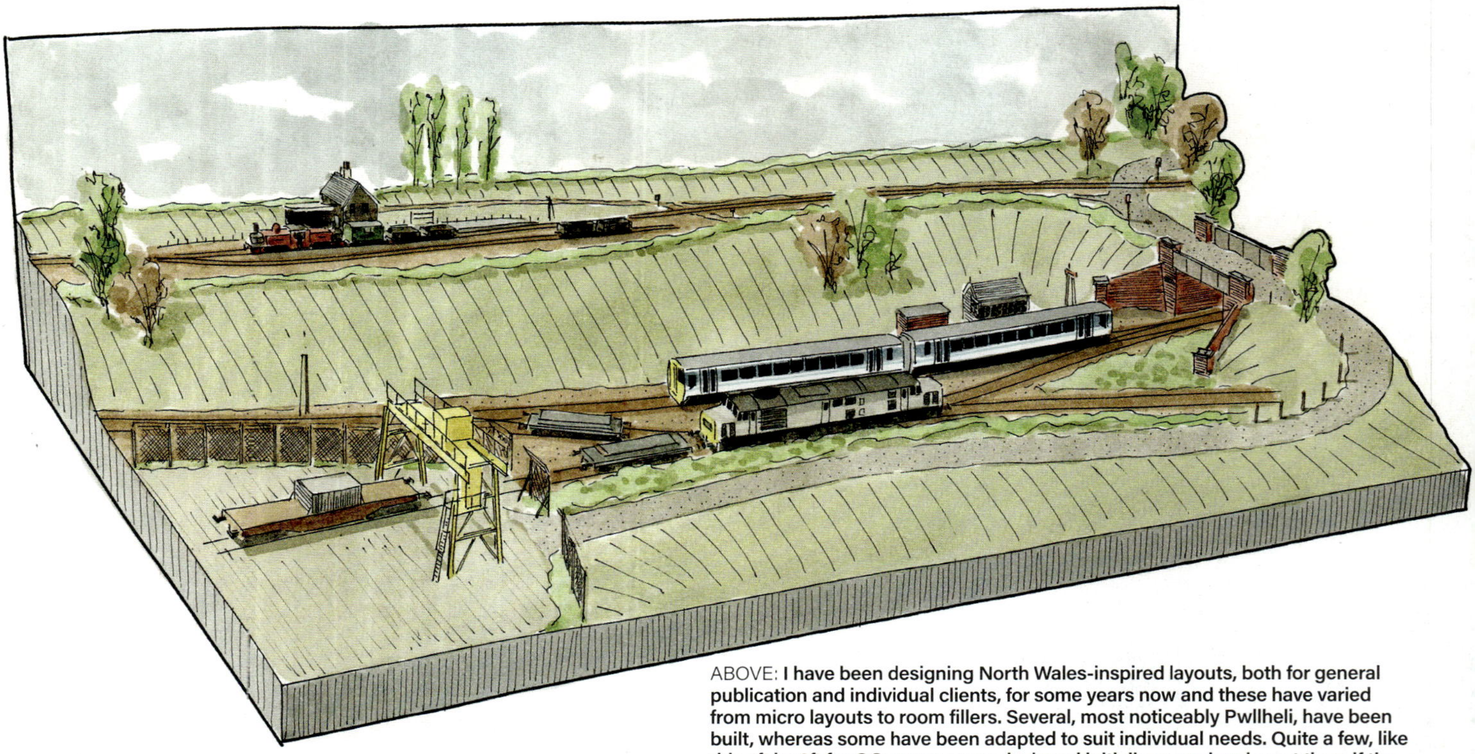

ABOVE: **I have been designing North Wales-inspired layouts, both for general publication and individual clients, for some years now and these have varied from micro layouts to room fillers. Several, most noticeably Pwllheli, have been built, whereas some have been adapted to suit individual needs. Quite a few, like this 4ft by 2ft for OO gauge, were designed initially as a micro layout then, if the opportunity arises, extended into a 'U', 'L' or oval format.**

Welcome to Modelling British Railways: North Wales. Each chapter covers a specific line with at a glance history and descriptions, location by location photo galleries, period postcards, trackplans and 3D illustrations. The content is designed to inspire modellers of all ages and skills, with several simplified Setrack entry-level plans that can be easily adapted to suit finer standards. The Back in Time and Over the Years sections show how scenes have changed and modellers striving for accuracy should be careful about what is included and what is left out. Loco and stock details for lesser known railways are included, whereas those for well-known lines are covered in other publications and online.

LEFT AND RIGHT: **Before we get into the detail, I want to go back in time. While born in Yorkshire, I began my lasting relationship with North Wales and fondly regard that 'We all have a place where we were born and one where we belong.' It all started with free family rail passes and ex Southern Terrier 32640, seen here at Eastleigh Sheds on August 3, 1964. The photo dates from before its departure to Pwllheli yard and then transfer to Butlin's camp at Penychain for permanent display.** Richard Inwood/Paul A Lunn Collection

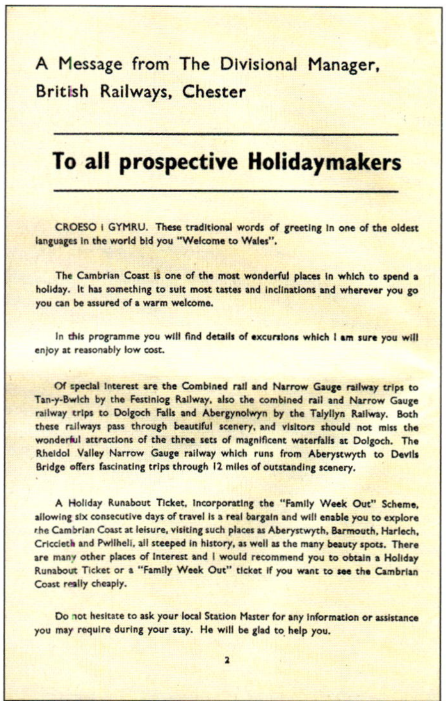

A Message from The Divisional Manager, British Railways, Chester

To all prospective Holidaymakers

CROESO I GYMRU. These traditional words of greeting in one of the oldest languages in the world bid you "Welcome to Wales".

The Cambrian Coast is one of the most wonderful places in which to spend a holiday. It has something to suit most tastes and inclinations and wherever you go you can be assured of a warm welcome.

In this programme you will find details of excursions which I am sure you will enjoy at reasonably low cost.

Of special interest are the Combined rail and Narrow Gauge railway trips to Tan-y-Bwlch by the Festiniog Railway, also the combined rail and Narrow Gauge railway trips to Dolgoch Falls and Abergynolwyn by the Talyllyn Railway. Both these railways pass through beautiful scenery, and visitors should not miss the wonderful attractions of the three sets of magnificent waterfalls at Dolgoch. The Rheidol Valley Narrow Gauge railway which runs from Aberystwyth to Devils Bridge offers fascinating trips through 12 miles of outstanding scenery.

A Holiday Runabout Ticket, incorporating the "Family Week Out" Scheme, allowing six consecutive days of travel is a real bargain and will enable you to explore the Cambrian Coast at leisure, visiting such places as Aberystwyth, Barmouth, Harlech, Criccieth and Pwllheli, all steeped in history, as well as the many beauty spots. There are many other places of interest and I would recommend you to obtain a Holiday Runabout Ticket or a "Family Week Out" ticket if you want to see the Cambrian Coast really cheaply.

Do not hesitate to ask your local Station Master for any information or assistance you may require during your stay. He will be glad to help you.

2

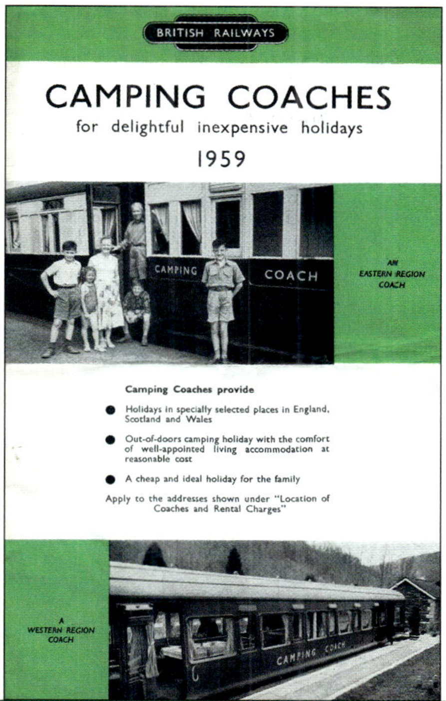

BRITISH RAILWAYS

CAMPING COACHES

for delightful inexpensive holidays

1959

Camping Coaches provide

- Holidays in specially selected places in England, Scotland and Wales
- Out-of-doors camping holiday with the comfort of well-appointed living accommodation at reasonable cost
- A cheap and ideal holiday for the family

Apply to the addresses shown under "Location of Coaches and Rental Charges"

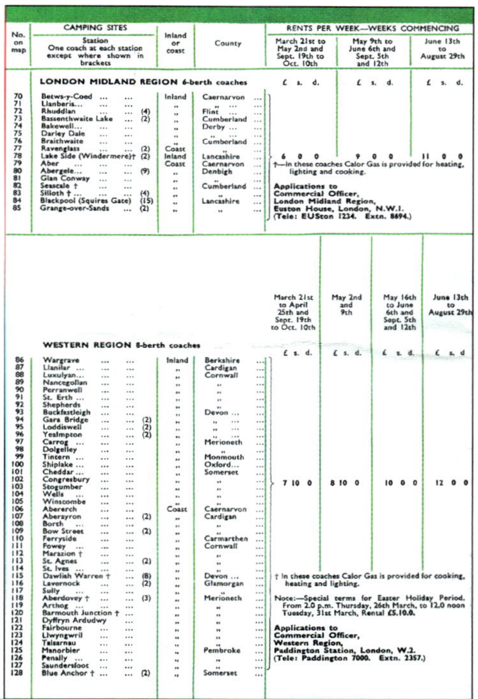

No. on map	CAMPING SITES: Station (One coach at each station except where shown in brackets)	Inland or coast	County	RENTS PER WEEK—WEEKS COMMENCING: March 21st to May 2nd and Sept. 19th to Oct. 10th	May 9th to June 6th and Sept. 5th and 12th	June 13th to August 29th
	LONDON MIDLAND REGION 6-berth coaches			£ s. d.	£ s. d.	£ s. d.
70	Betws-y-Coed	Inland	Caernarvon ...			
71	Llanberis...	"	"			
72	Rhuddlan ... ... (4)	"	Flint			
73	Bassenthwaite Lake ... (2)	"	Cumberland ...			
74	Bakewell...	"	Derby			
75	Darley Dale	"	"			
76	Braithwaite	"	Cumberland ...			
77	Ravenglass ... ... (2)	Coast	" ...			
78	Lake Side (Windermere)† (2)	Inland	Lancashire ...	6 0 0	9 0 0	11 0 0
79	Aber	Coast	Caernarvon ...			
80	Abergele... ... ... (9)	"	Denbigh ...			
81	Glan Conway	"	" ...			
82	Seascale †	"	Cumberland ...			
83	Silloth † ... ... (4)	"	" ...			
84	Blackpool (Squires Gate) (15)	"	Lancashire ...			
85	Grange-over-Sands ... (2)	"	" ...			

†—In these coaches Calor Gas is provided for heating, lighting and cooking.

Applications to Commercial Officer, London Midland Region, Euston House, London, N.W.1. (Tele: EUSton 1234. Extn. 8694.)

No. on map	Station	Inland or coast	County	March 21st to April 25th and Sept. 19th to Oct. 10th	May 2nd and 9th	May 16th to June 6th and Sept. 5th and 12th	June 13th to August 29th
	WESTERN REGION 8-berth coaches			£ s. d.	£ s. d.	£ s. d.	£ s. d
86	Wargrave	Inland	Berkshire ...				
87	Llanilar	"	Cardigan ...				
88	Luxulyan...	"	Cornwall ...				
89	Nancegollan	"	" ...				
90	Perranwell	"	" ...				
91	St. Erth	"	" ...				
92	Shepherds	"	" ...				
93	Buckfastleigh	"	Devon				
94	Gara Bridge ... ... (2)	"	"				
95	Loddiswell ... ... (2)	"	"				
96	Yealmpton ... ... (2)	"	"				
97	Carrog	"	Merioneth ...				
98	Dolgelley	"	" ...				
99	Tintern	"	Monmouth ...				
100	Shiplake	"	Oxford... ...				
101	Cheddar	"	Somerset ...				
102	Congresbury	"	" ...	7 10 0	8 10 0	10 0 0	12 0 0
103	Stogumber	"	" ...				
104	Wells	"	" ...				
105	Winscombe	"	" ...				
106	Abererch	Coast	Caernarvon ...				
107	Aberayron ... ... (2)	"	Cardigan ...				
108	Borth	"	" ...				
109	Bow Street ... ... (2)	"	" ...				
110	Ferryside	"	Carmarthen ...				
111	Fowey	"	Cornwall ...				
112	Marazion †	"	" ...				
113	St. Agnes ... ... (2)	"	" ...				
114	St. Ives	"	" ...				
115	Dawlish Warren † ... (8)	"	Devon				
116	Lavernock ... ... (2)	"	Glamorgan ...				
117	Sully	"	" ...				
118	Aberdovey † ... ... (3)	"	Merioneth ...				
119	Arthog	"	" ...				
120	Barmouth Junction † ...	"	" ...				
121	Dyffryn Ardudwy ...	"	" ...				
122	Fairbourne	"	" ...				
123	Llwyngwril	"	" ...				
124	Talsarnau	"	" ...				
125	Manorbier	"	Pembroke ...				
126	Penally	"	" ...				
127	Saundersfoot	"	" ...				
128	Blue Anchor † ... ... (2)	"	Somerset ...				

† In these coaches Calor Gas is provided for cooking, heating and lighting.

Note:—Special terms for Easter Holiday Period. From 2.0 p.m. Thursday, 26th March, to 12.0 noon Tuesday, 31st March, Rental £5.10.0.

Applications to Commercial Officer, Western Region, Paddington Station, London, W.2. (Tele: Paddington 7000. Extn. 2357.)

ABOVE: **Always aware of holiday hotspots, BR made every effort to attract visitors, even those who had to pay! Camping coaches played a huge part in that process and particularly relevant in this bookazine are the ones from the London Midland and Western regions, as you will see in due course.**

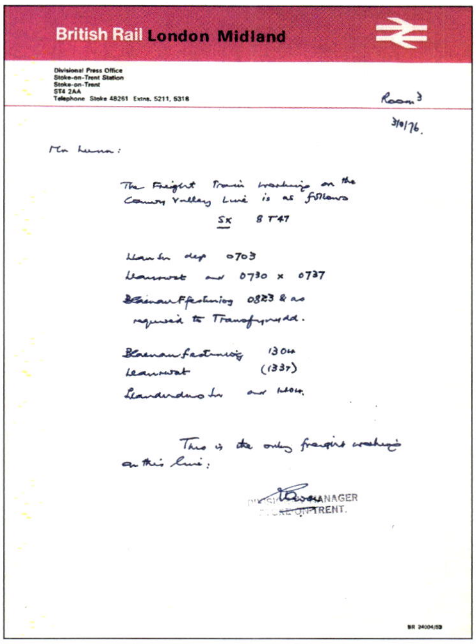

British Rail London Midland

Divisional Press Office
Stoke-on-Trent Station
Stoke-on-Trent
ST4 2AA
Telephone Stoke 48261 Extns. 5211, 5318

Room 3

3/10/76.

The Freight Train working on the Conwy Valley Line is as follows

SX 8T47

Llandudno Jn dep 0703
Llanrwst arr 0730 x 0737
Blaenau Ffestiniog 0823 & as required to Trawsfynydd.

Blaenau Ffestiniog 1304
Llanrwst (1337)
Llandudno Jn arr 1404.

This is the only freight working on this line;

...ANAGER
...-ON-TRENT.

BR 24004/53

ABOVE, RIGHT AND FAR RIGHT: **I could not have done any of this without help, particularly my wife Melenie, who acted as co-researcher, route and location finder, proof reader and provided so much more essential support. My thanks too to BR and some of the most welcoming railway staff in the UK, enabling photo opportunities, train timings, cab rides and visits. Thanks are also due to Jonathan Buckie for the photos of his layout Pwllheli.**

LEFT: **The right camera for the job?**
There were mixed results with my dad's Ensign and passed-on Kodak Brownie, but Halina Paulette Electrics were a step in the right direction. I had two, always loaded and ready to go; one with superb Ilford FP4 film, the other Agfa slides. By the 1990s, I had progressed to an outstanding Olympus OM10 and was saddened when the shutter gave up the ghost. I never got on well with a Nikon SLR, great kit but so bulky. Then there was the Apple 14 phone, no kit bag and all the paraphernalia that goes with it, just great photos, real and model, almost every time.

RIGHT: **Bucket list**
Fast forward to 2023 and time for some highly focussed research, plugging gaps in my collection and a first, 'bucket list' ride over Barmouth Bridge and beyond. This all recalling scenic vistas, freight trains, narrow gauge interchanges, expired infrastructure, and visualising prototype-inspired layouts. Sit back and enjoy the ride with detailed routes, many previously unpublished photos, 16 new track plans and several 3D images, all ideal for modellers and enthusiasts alike.

Through the landscape

If modelling North Wales, consideration must be given to the area's geographical features as much as the railways to ensure a convincing whole is created.

Before getting into actual routes, I particularly want to draw attention to the often unique landscapes of North Wales, these varying from vast coastal vistas and flat plains to valleys, hills, and mountains, some of considerable height and volume. I guess what I am saying is that Wales needs to really look like Wales. To aid this process, this section features a selection of relevant and inspirational landscapes.

We often stereotype settings, driven by our layout design and spaces left behind after the track has been laid. It can result in a planted-on look, rather than a trackbed cutting through existing terrain. This is compounded by flat top baseboards which only allow land mass to rise upward and not below rail height, therefore losing some element of realism. Resolving this takes time but is worth it, especially for Welsh mud flats and marshland.

With buildings, we all shop in the same marketplace, and this is true of scenic treatments too, especially ground cover, readymade trees and so on. We plonk and place, often without much forethought, and I suspect rarely looking at real locations for accurate inspiration.

All of the photos taken by me were either from public vantage points or with permission from on-site staff. Having gained permission, I always make sure I behave in a safe and respectful way, both for my benefit and for that of others, especially railway staff. I do not condone trespassing on the railway for any reason.

RIGHT: **Croeso I Gymru** Welsh would be my second language, if I had time to learn, and while I can pronounce a few short sentences and railway location names (Pwllheli, Machynlleth and the like), the rest I am afraid to admit are read phonetically and nothing like they should sound, although it does help my spelling on the written page! This is a conundrum that many have struggled with and indeed the likes of British Rail have made efforts to encourage understanding, as can be seen from a 1950s/60s promotional brochure. I say this to explain that my long-in-the-tooth experience has seen names come and go and that I sometimes use one or the other or both in the same sentence. Thus, my use of Welsh and English versions is for historical relevance and that no offence is meant by this method.

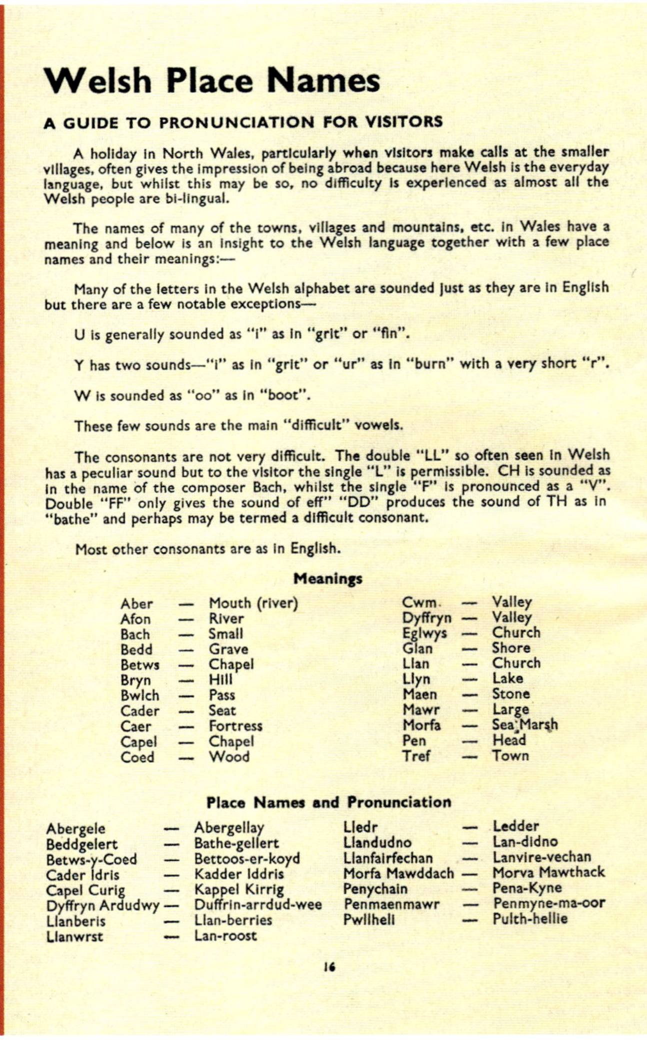

Welsh Place Names

A GUIDE TO PRONUNCIATION FOR VISITORS

A holiday in North Wales, particularly when visitors make calls at the smaller villages, often gives the impression of being abroad because here Welsh is the everyday language, but whilst this may be so, no difficulty is experienced as almost all the Welsh people are bi-lingual.

The names of many of the towns, villages and mountains, etc. in Wales have a meaning and below is an insight to the Welsh language together with a few place names and their meanings:—

Many of the letters in the Welsh alphabet are sounded just as they are in English but there are a few notable exceptions—

U is generally sounded as "i" as in "grit" or "fin".

Y has two sounds—"i" as in "grit" or "ur" as in "burn" with a very short "r".

W is sounded as "oo" as in "boot".

These few sounds are the main "difficult" vowels.

The consonants are not very difficult. The double "LL" so often seen in Welsh has a peculiar sound but to the visitor the single "L" is permissible. CH is sounded as in the name of the composer Bach, whilst the single "F" is pronounced as a "V". Double "FF" only gives the sound of eff" "DD" produces the sound of TH as in "bathe" and perhaps may be termed a difficult consonant.

Most other consonants are as in English.

Meanings

Aber	—	Mouth (river)	Cwm	—	Valley
Afon	—	River	Dyffryn	—	Valley
Bach	—	Small	Eglwys	—	Church
Bedd	—	Grave	Glan	—	Shore
Betws	—	Chapel	Llan	—	Church
Bryn	—	Hill	Llyn	—	Lake
Bwlch	—	Pass	Maen	—	Stone
Cader	—	Seat	Mawr	—	Large
Caer	—	Fortress	Morfa	—	Sea Marsh
Capel	—	Chapel	Pen	—	Head
Coed	—	Wood	Tref	—	Town

Place Names and Pronunciation

Abergele	—	Abergellay	Lledr	—	Ledder
Beddgelert	—	Bathe-gellert	Llandudno	—	Lan-didno
Betws-y-Coed	—	Bettoos-er-koyd	Llanfairfechan	—	Lanvire-vechan
Cader Idris	—	Kadder Iddris	Morfa Mawddach	—	Morva Mawthack
Capel Curig	—	Kappel Kirrig	Penychain	—	Pena-Kyne
Dyffryn Ardudwy	—	Duffrin-arrdud-wee	Penmaenmawr	—	Penmyne-ma-oor
Llanberis	—	Llan-berries	Pwllheli	—	Pulth-hellie
Llanwrst	—	Lan-roost			

16

LEFT: **A Class 24-hauled freight from Machynlleth to Pwllheli, made up of eight gunpowder vans, nine ventilated vans, three 16-ton minerals and a BR standard brake, is seen south of Fairbourne station on September 1, 1975. Note the wild grass and gorse down to a rocky beach and contrasting rough stone walls, some in disrepair.**

ABOVE: **Gateway**
37428 at the southern end of Shrewsbury station with Severn Bridge Junction signal box between the lines; left to Wellington and right to North Wales. While many North Wales trains are or have been quite local, the area has been served from much further afield; Chester, Wrexham, Shrewsbury, London and one route, now closed, from Carmarthen via Aberystwyth. There have been several named trains, such as the *Cambrian Coast Express*, *The Snowdonian*, *The Welsh Chieftain*, a variety of *Land Cruises* and the *Cambrian Radio Cruise*, bringing a certain style to the experience. It may well be that some readers with considerable space, or are happy with N gauge, would consider one of the major stations above, together with a through station like Welshpool, Machynlleth or Barmouth and terminating at Aberystwyth or Pwllheli.

ABOVE: **A path from near Glandyfi station provides the only access to Dovey Junction. Note there are wide ranging textures in this winter scene and that the adjacent land is below track level.**

ABOVE: **Across the Dovey Estuary on September 1, 1975, with a barely discernible short freight lost in the contrasting grandeur of marshy coastal plains and distant hills. You would need substantial baseboard depth to model such terrain and suggest 3D modelling, in richer greens, up to the hills and tree line behind the train. Distant hills, in grey-brown and a hint of green, should be represented with a photographic backscene.**

ABOVE: **Between Aberdovey and Gogarth Halt, there is a section of track along a shallow ledge, retained and protected by some impressive, yet basic, stonework. The sea and river estuaries play an important part on the western coastline and, wherever modelling space permits, should be included for a locational statement and visual effect.** Richard Inwood/Paul A Lunn Collection

ABOVE: **About as short a train as you can get, close to Black Rock Halt on an early misty morning on March 22, 1976. It is an exposed area, prone to flooding and with sparse grass and gorse, so would require careful representation.**

ABOVE: **I have always been a bit critical of the archetypal summer's day that so many of us seem to represent and, in more recent times, have been encouraging others, and myself, to consider alternates. The weather in North Wales is unpredictable and yet can be quite dramatic as this image of Barmouth Bridge, with almost silhouetted hills, shows on July 31, 2023.**

ABOVE: **This is a particular favourite of mine, with 46443 harping back to what steam days looked like. Taken on August 3, 1987, it is the contrast, colours, composition of horizontal lines, and various textures that does it for me.**

RIGHT: **Depending on period and location modelled, some can be hard-surfaced and monotone in appearance, as this study at Blaenau Ffestiniog shows.**

ABOVE: **An almost entirely organic scene: fences and walls undulate, every road and farm track weaves its way, sometimes to avoid impassable terrain, and surfaces vary from short grass to rocky outcrops, not a flat piece of baseboard in sight!**

ABOVE: **Ethically questionable in real life but outstandingly dramatic as a model. It is a vista best created in N gauge, perhaps recycling life expired roofing slates, well and truly crushed to an acceptable scale.**

ABOVE: **Even when you are in close proximity to a landscape, it is worth considering all the elements, however small. Besides the obvious textures and greying distant hills, I want to question why ivy has grown at equally spaced intervals on the boarded building? Perhaps because of an easier foothold, maybe someone put mesh up to encourage growth. Honestly, I do not know the answer, I just want us to observe in more detail, then replicate what we see, for improved interest and accuracy.**

ABOVE: **Sometimes the way a landscape appears might surprise us in unusual composition, texture and location, like this solitary skeletal bush in a stream between Rhys Gog and Llanfyllin on March 21, 1976. Note the distant railway bridge.**

Key to all trackplans

Throughout this bookazine, each gridded square on all model track plans represents 1ft in 4mm scale, regardless of track gauge. All rigid geometry curves are second radius unless stated, otherwise with 1, 3 or 4 on plan indicating first, third and fourth radii respectively. YP indicates a rigid geometry 'Y' point while Y indicates the curve that matches a 'Y' point. ISO indicates an isolating track for DC with A to B, C to D and so on indicating a length of gradient.

Pwllheli to Porthmadog

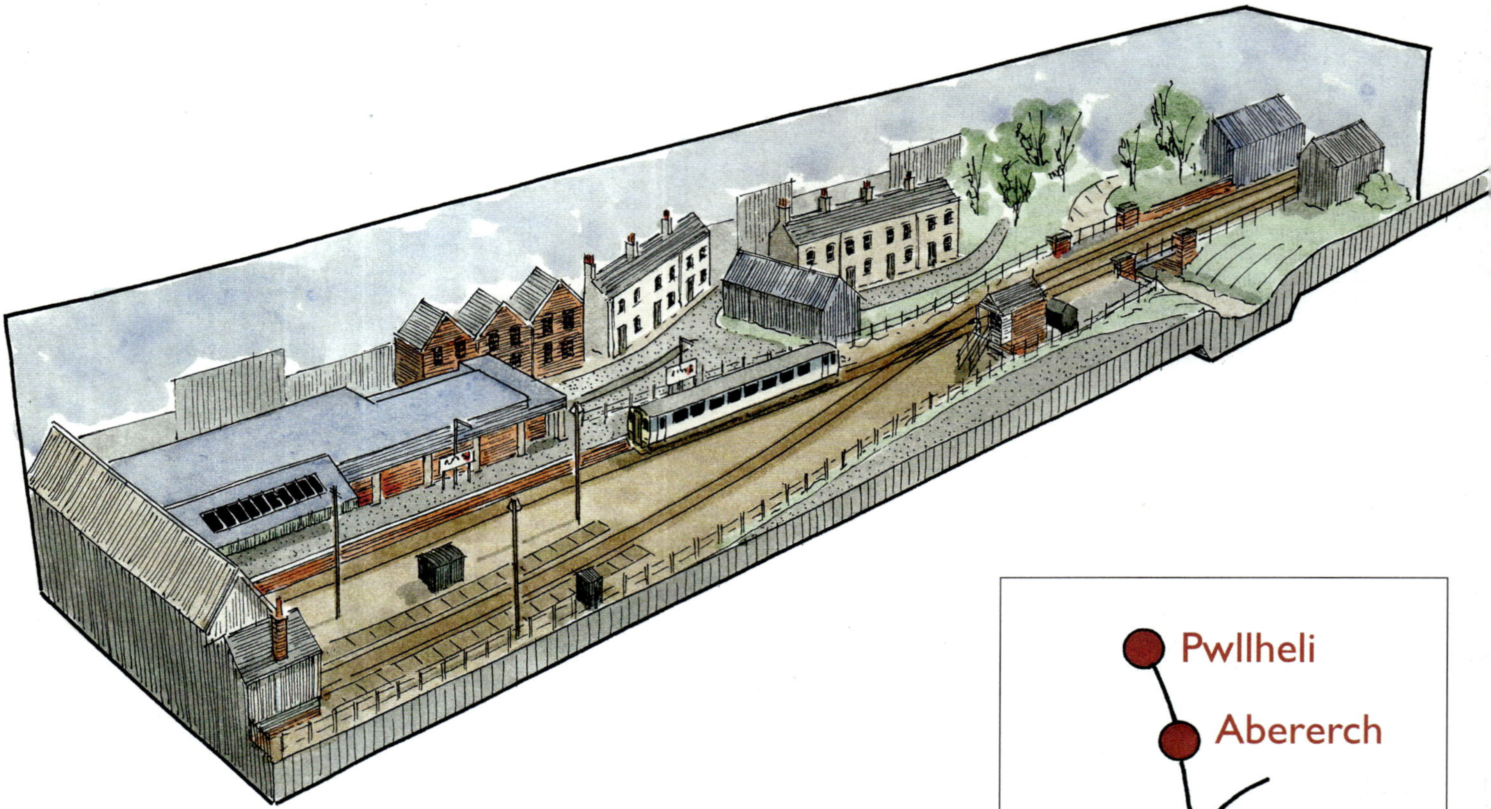

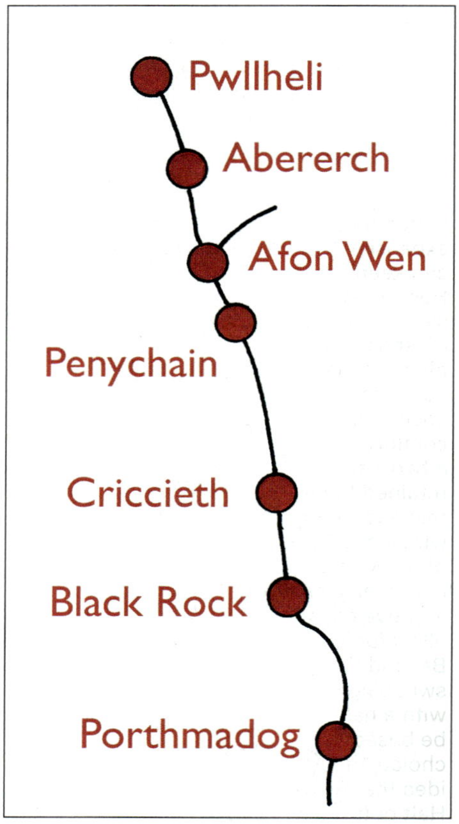

History and description at a glance

This is a scenic jewel, hugging or close to one of the most dramatic coastlines in the UK. There were standard gauge junctions at Afon Wen and Barmouth, three narrow gauge interchanges at Porthmadog alone, and stations varying from a simple wooden trestle halt to the most substantial of structures. The line has been continuously marketed as serving tourist hotspots and, despite attempts at closure, it is currently seeing significant regeneration.

In steam days, ex-GWR and BR standard locos plied their way along the route, not only for tourists but school children as well and a wide range of freight commodities. This culminated in diesel days, with mainly coal and explosives from Penrhyndeudraeth.

As a line with ageing infrastructure, it has been plagued with problems, most noticeably at Barmouth Bridge, but over the years decaying halts, like Gogarth, and the demise of signals and signal boxes have become a distant memory.

Location by location

Pwllheli station both in its original and modified form has always caught my eye as an attractive, potentially minimum space, prototype and if you interpret it as an expanding modern railhead, there will be sufficient operating interest too. The first of the two 3D illustrations shows a much compressed version requiring one single slip at the station throat, while the second side-on illustration features an added fictitious railhead in the right foreground. A detailed account of modelling Pwllheli appeared in *Making tracks* by Paul A Lunn from Atlantic Publishers (ISBN 9781902827223) and available from paullunndzine@gmail.com.

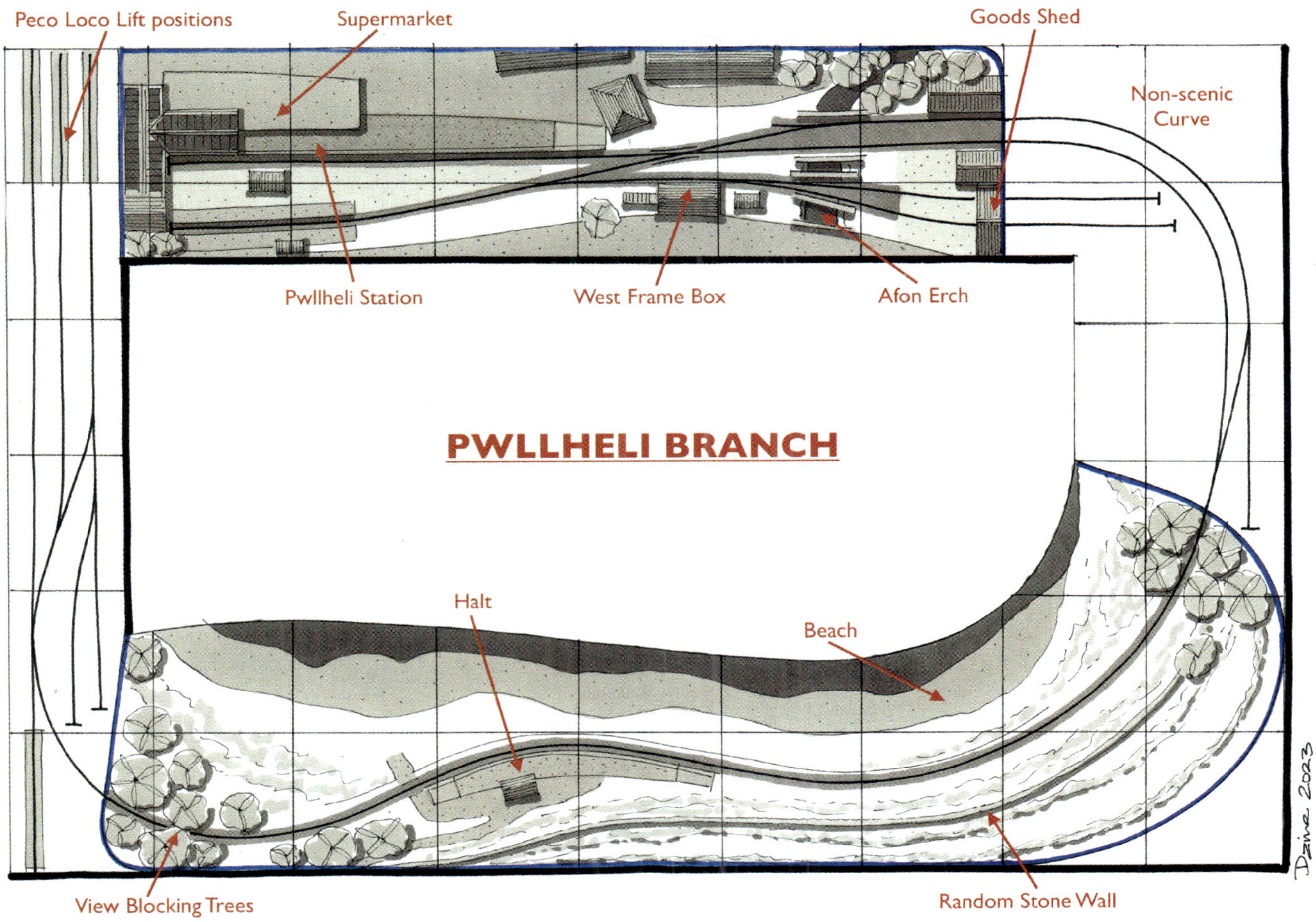

I often harp on about factoring in possible expansion from the start, that way you can keep any modifications to a minimum. Here, I have taken the plan from the second 3D and enlarged it to fit a 9ft by 6ft space. The loop and platform just about accommodate a three-coach train, although comfortably manages a two-car DMU. I have retained the fictional railhead sidings, each with a short section of track onto the non-scenic section to improve capacity and allow for load removal. Beyond the loop is a sweeping coastal run with a halt that could be based on any of your choice, though I like the idea that Black Rock Halt gets a new lease of life, to capitalise on the outstanding nearby beach. If more space allows, particularly in length, I will use it to increase the main platform.

Simplified Setrack

Pwllheli is easy to represent at entry-level using rigid geometry track and with fictitious railhead sidings again for increased operation. The design is set for late steam/early diesel, hence the island platform with track on both sides. Maximum train length for the station and fiddle yard is three coaches, slightly more if you use a second loco to release an inbound train. The loop is capable of handling a short freight train or a released loco.

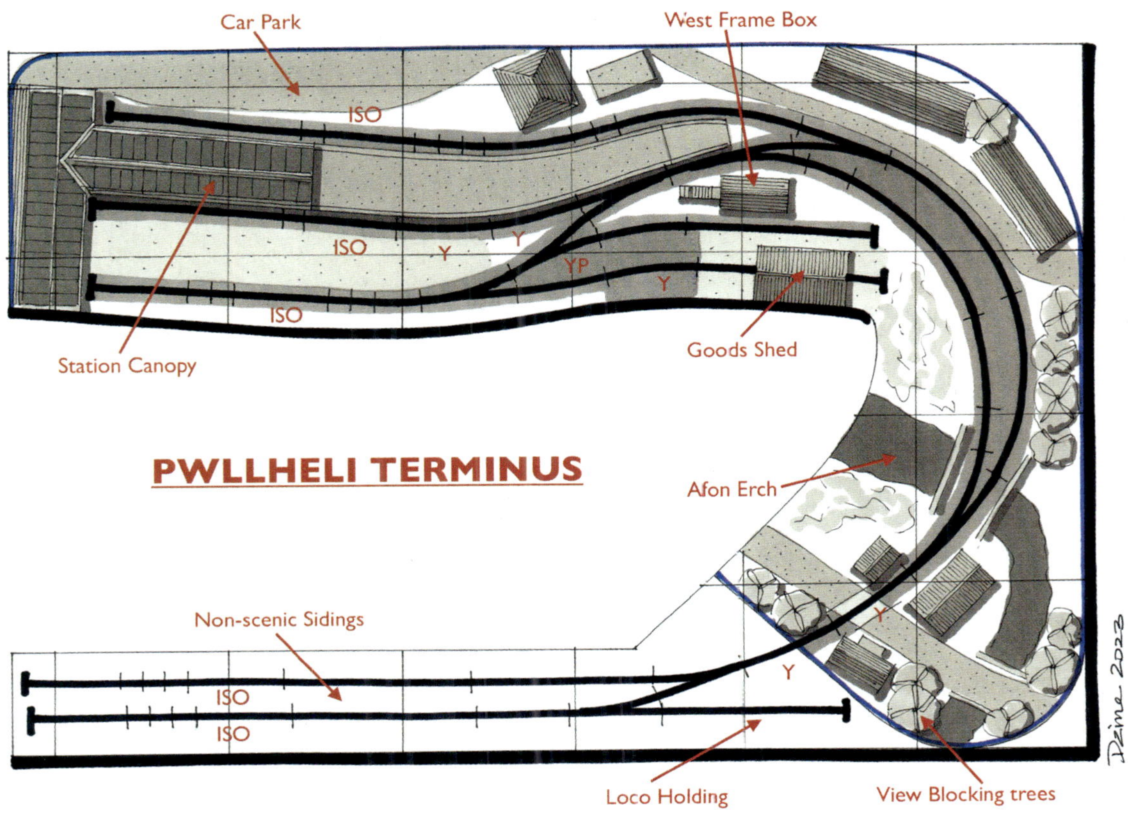

ABOVE AND LEFT: **Certainly, my design seems to have been well received and has been the basis for several variations, some more fictional and others quite faithful, like this finer scale example from Jonathan Buckie.**

LEFT AND RIGHT: **The accompanying 1986 pamphlet and 1950s/60s timetable extract focus on holiday hotspots; Porthmadog giving access to the Ffestiniog Railway, Barmouth, Criccieth and Harlech for impressively situated castles, Butlin's Holiday Camp at Penychain, miniature railway, Fairbourne and Tywyn for the Talyllyn Railway. Somethings never change and, even these days, you still have to advise the guard/conductor of setting down at certain unstaffed halts.**

Principal Train Services to:—

Aberystwyth—Barmouth—Harlech—Portmadoc

Criccieth—Penychain—Pwllheli

Mondays to Fridays, 13th June to 2nd September, 1966

FROM									
PWLLHELI	dep.	0745	0820	1020	1310	—	1609	1740	1830
ABBERERCH HALT	„	0750	—	1025	1315	—	Z	Z	—
PENYCHAIN	„	0754	0828	1028	1318	—	1617	1748	1838
CRICCIETH	„	0803	0837	1037	1327	—	1626	1757	1848
PORTMADOC	„	0814	0848	1050	1338	—	1638	1810	1900
MINFFORDD	„	0818	—	1054	1342	—	1641	1814	1904
PENRHYNDEUDRAETH ...	„	0823	0856	1058	1347	—	1645	1829	1909
LLANDECWYN HALT	„	0827	—	Z	1351	—	Z	1832	—
TALSARNAU	„	0830	—	1104	1354	—	1652	1836	1916
TYGWYN HALT	„	0833	—	Z	1357	—	1654	1838	—
HARLECH	„	0841	0907	1112	1403	—	1700	1844	1923
LLANDANWG HALT	„	0847	—	Z	1409	—	Z	—	—
LLANBEDR & P.	„	0849	—	1120	1411	—	1712	1852	1931
TALWRN BACH HALT ...	„	0852	—	Z	1414	—	1715	1855	—
DYFFRYN ARDUDWY	„	0857	—	1127	1419	—	1720	1900	1938
TALYBONT HALT	„	0901	—	1131	1423	—	1724	1904	1942
LLANABER HALT	„	0905	—	1135	1428	—	—	—	—
BARMOUTH	arr	0909	0926	1141	1432	—	1732	1911	1951
BARMOUTH	dep.	—	0930	1156	1440	1525	1744	—	1955
MORFA MAWDDACH	„	—	0935	1201	1445	1530	1749	—	2000
FAIRBOURNE	„	—	0938	1205	1448	1534	1753	—	2005
LLWYNGWRIL	„	—	0947	1214	1456	1543	1801	—	2014
LLANDECWYN HALT	„	—	Z	1219	1501	1548	Z	—	—
TONFANAU	„	—	0955	1223	1506	1552	1810	—	2022
TOWYN	„	—	1000	1230	1513	1557	1817	—	2029
ABERDOVEY	„	—	1007	1238	1521	1607	1824	—	2036
PENHELIG HALT	„	—	1011	1241	1524	1611	1827	—	2039
ABERTAFOL HALT	„	—	Z	Z	Z	Z	Z	—	—
GOGARTH HALT	„	—	Z	Z	Z	1619	Z	—	—
DOVEY JUNCTION	arr.	—	1026	1256	1541	1624	1841	—	—
MACHYNLLETH	arr.	—	1039	1310	1605	1632	1851	—	2059
MACHYNLLETH	„	—	1020	1250	1633	1633	1830	—	2207
DOVEY JUNCTION	arr.	—	1027	1257	1639	1639	1837	—	—
DOVEY JUNCTION	dep.	—	1030	1303	1640	1640	1846	—	—
BORTH	„	—	1043	1316	16*53	1653	1900	—	22†27
ABERYSTWYTH	arr.	—	1102	1335	17*10	1710	1918	—	22†46

NOTES

Heavy figures denote through services.
Light figures denote connecting services.
†—Change at Machynlleth.
*—Passengers for Borth and Aberystwyth may travel via Machynlleth if they wish to do so.
Z—Set down only on notice being given to the Guard at previous stopping station, and picks up on notice being given to the Driver.

THE SERVICES SHOWN ON THIS PAGE ARE NOT A COMPLETE LIST OF TRAINS SERVING THE CAMBRIAN COAST RESORTS, CERTAIN OTHER SERVICES TO AND FROM PLACES OF INTEREST ARE SHOWN ON OTHER PAGES OF THIS BOOKLET BUT FOR FULL DETAILS OF ALL SERVICES, PLEASE CONSULT THE CAMBRIAN COAST AND NORTH WALES SECTIONAL TIME-TABLE ON SALE AT YOUR HOLIDAY STATION — PRICE SIXPENCE.

12

Over the years

While researching history is helpful in any prototype endeavour, images always provide the best resource for getting the feel of a place, not only in terms of composition but in how things have changed.

ABOVE: **Looking towards Barmouth, 75004 heads a short train past Pwllheli West Frame Signal Box on August 27, 1964. Trains with a limited number of coaches are ideal for a highly compressed layout design.** Richard Inwood/Paul A Lunn Collection

ABOVE: **80099 departs from the platform bay at Pwllheli on August 27, 1964, this later succumbing to a supermarket and car park. Note the fine old timber posted signals.** Richard Inwood/Paul A Lunn Collection

ABOVE: **Fast forward to March 22, 1976, finds a Class 101 waiting time. Of note is a grounded coach body, possibly for cleaners, unusual and rarely modelled station lamp bases, and a solitary ventilated van, up against the loading dock platform.**

ABOVE: **1986 and the end of the line, although there had always been a desire to extend to Porth Dinlleyn on the coast. There is much to commend this scene in terms of surfaces and textures and indeed colour palette. I particularly like the heavily oil stained track.**

ABOVE: **Getting right up to date on July 30, 2023, and 158835 and 158829 have been stabled here overnight and cleaners are already working on the latter. The traincrew have just arrived and it will not be long before the first Sunday service is on its way. Note the replacement supermarket building and how it obliterates part of the original canopy.**

ABOVE: **A stark contrast between the somewhat dated 'modern' stock and several original features, including bullhead rail, weather-worn sleepers, and ex-BR(W) bufferstop. Make sure you pick what is right for your modelled time period as transitional years can always create oddities.**

Building – in the detail

BELOW: **Pwllheli station building dates from 1909 and is a 'T' shaped arrangement with the main building and adjacent concourse at a right angle to the main line. It is a timber structure with felted roof and brick chimneys, with all the hallmarks of a light railway!**

LEFT: **The main concourse is a substantial essay in girders and beams. How much you would need to model depends on what you can see, especially for the expansive run in pre-supermarket days.**

LEFT: **Pwllheli's solitary island platform was originally quite wide with an equally wide canopy span either side of the substantial columns. DMUs were introduced in January 1965 with this four-car unit forming the 10.25 to Machynlleth on March 22, 1976.**

Pwllheli West Frame signal box

A McKenzie and Holland, Dutton type 2 signal box, situated on the coastal side of the tracks just beyond the station platform and was downgraded to a four lever frame (originally 40 levers). The substantial structure, despite an air of dereliction, has stood the test of time, particularly given its exposed location. My survey dates from 1986, although the scale elevations were constructed at a later date, largely from measuring bricks. This assumes that one brick plus one vertical mortar joint equals to 9½ inches. In the last couple of years, the box has been fully refurbished, still retaining its four lever frame, some internal furnishings and protective meshing to a number of windows.

FRONT ELEVATION

1' 2' 3' 4' 5' 6' 7' 8' 9' 10'

REAR ELEVATION

WEST ELEVATION

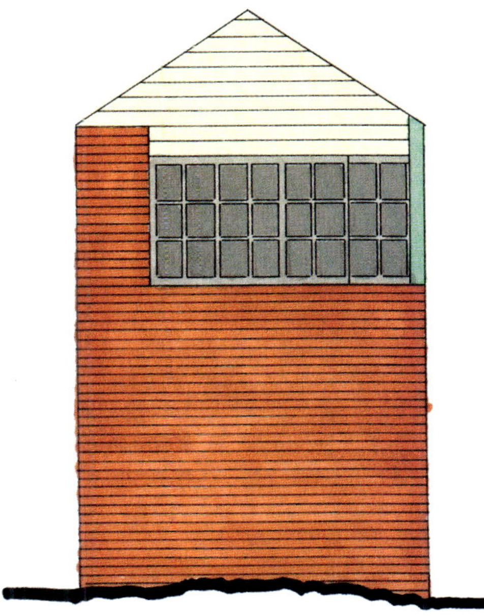

EAST ELEVATION

Pwllheli East signal box

LEFT, BELOW LEFT AND BELOW RIGHT: **Pwllheli East signal box had a 23 lever frame and was built in 1935 to replace a Cambrian box. The East box was taken out of use in 1976, converted to a ground frame and has since been demolished. The original 1867 station, accessed by Station Road, was nearby together with a small goods yard, a loco shed measuring 100ft by 45ft and a turntable, which is now at the West Somerset Railway.**

ABOVE: **Abererch station originally had a slate-cladded crossing keeper's house adjacent to an unstaffed platform. It was upgraded to a staffed station in 1933 and reduced to an unstaffed halt in 1956. The platforms were low and sets of steps were used to access trains. There was a waiting room and small office in a wooden hut, a solitary siding, and a three-lever ground frame in a hut, adjacent to the level crossing. All of this was subsequently replaced by the modern structure seen on July 30, 2023.**

ABOVE AND RIGHT: **Afon Wen station** was built purely as a junction for both GWR Cambrian and LNWR Caernarfon lines, and with little evidence of life around the place, it was somewhat desolate. The main station building was on an island platform and had a licensed refreshment room. There were two footbridges, a brick and timber signal box with a 75 lever frame, a turntable removed in the 1930s, two water tanks, a stationmaster's bungalow, and a row of railway workers terrace houses nearby. The station was opened on September 2, 1867, and closed in 1964. For modellers, junctions always bring added interest due to greater operational value and the significance of connecting trains. Modelling Afon Wen was described, in considerable detail, by Stephen Rabone and Trevor Ridley in *Layout Designs for Operation* by Atlantic Publishers (ISBN 9781902827148).

Butlin's Pwllheli Holiday Camp at Penychain

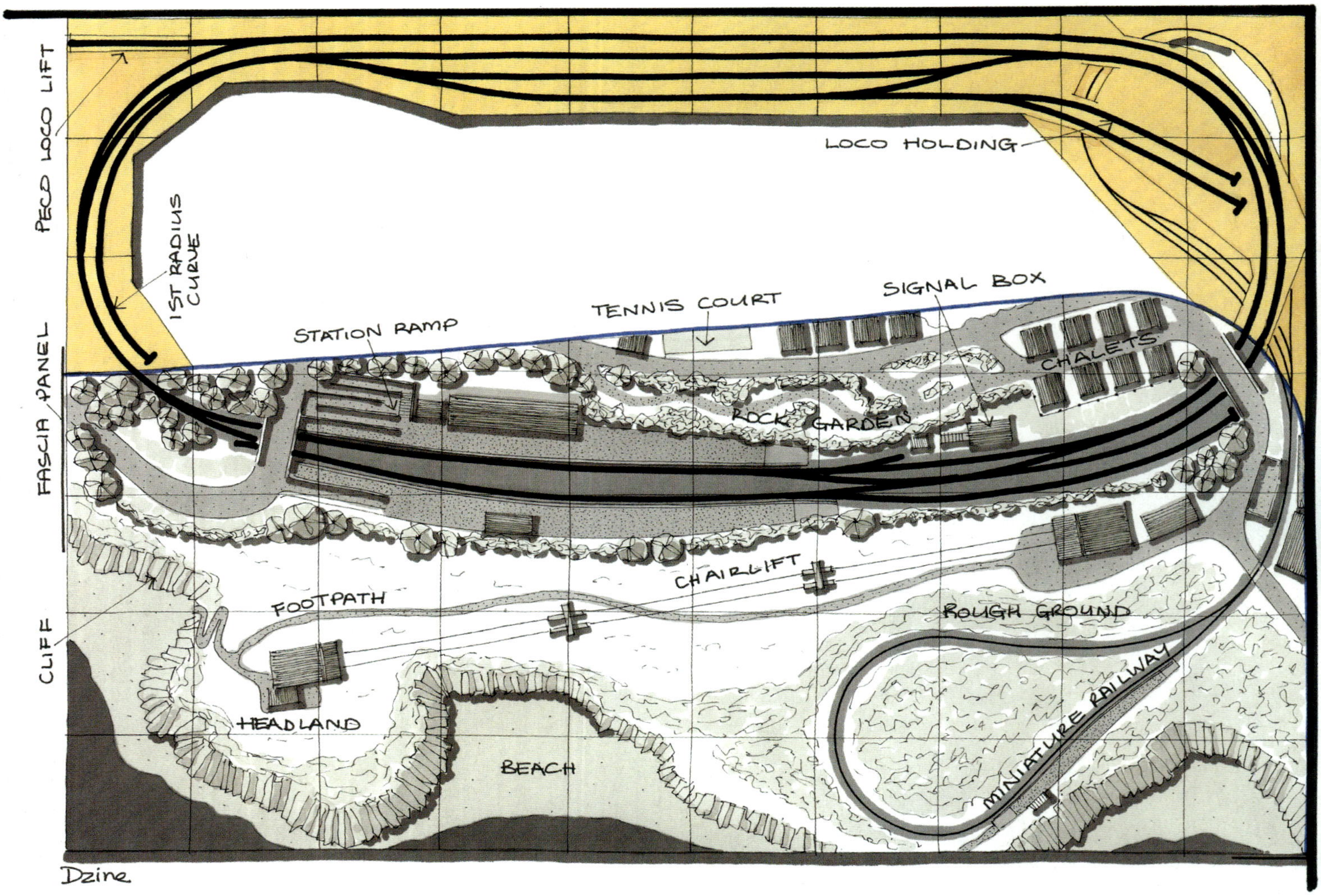

TOP AND ABOVE: **The accompanying 10ft by 7ft trackplan includes all the key components, namely the BR station, Butlin's camp, chair lift, miniature railway, and coastal headland, compressing them into a relatively small area. In doing so, there are advantages such as the inclusion of so many features, especially the dramatic headland, and of course disadvantages, namely a reduction in train length from a prototype ten coaches down to four. Please note the plan is for OO gauge and uses Peco Setrack for the non-scenic curves. The accompanying photo is of a Butlin's miniature railway train, preserved at the Midland Railway - Butterley.**

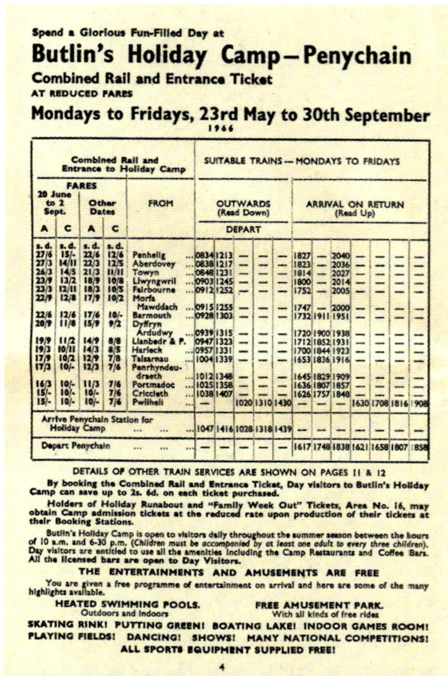

Spend a Glorious Fun-Filled Day at

Butlin's Holiday Camp—Penychain

Combined Rail and Entrance Ticket

AT REDUCED FARES

Mondays to Fridays, 23rd May to 30th September

1966

Combined Rail and Entrance to Holiday Camp					SUITABLE TRAINS—MONDAYS TO FRIDAYS											
FARES 20 June to 2 Sept.		FARES Other Dates		FROM	OUTWARDS (Read Down) DEPART					ARRIVAL ON RETURN (Read Up)						
A	C	A	C													
s. d.	s. d.	s. d.	s. d.													
27/6	15/-	22/6	12/6	Penhelig ...	0834	1213	—	—	—	1827	—	2040	—	—	—	—
27/3	14/11	22/3	12/5	Aberdovey ...	0838	1217	—	—	—	1823	—	2036	—	—	—	—
26/3	14/5	21/3	11/11	Towyn ...	0848	1231	—	—	—	1814	—	2027	—	—	—	—
23/9	13/2	18/9	10/8	Llwyngwril ...	0903	1245	—	—	—	1800	—	2014	—	—	—	—
23/3	12/11	18/3	10/5	Fairbourne ...	0912	1252	—	—	—	1752	—	2005	—	—	—	—
22/9	12/8	17/9	10/2	Morfa Mawddach ...	0915	1255	—	—	—	1747	—	2000	—	—	—	—
22/6	12/6	17/6	10/-	Barmouth ...	0928	1303	—	—	—	1732	1911	1951	—	—	—	—
20/9	11/8	15/9	9/2	Dyffryn Ardudwy ...	0939	1315	—	—	—	1720	1900	1938	—	—	—	—
19/9	11/2	14/9	8/8	Llanbedr & P.	0947	1323	—	—	—	1712	1852	1931	—	—	—	—
19/3	10/11	14/3	8/5	Harlech ...	0957	1331	—	—	—	1700	1844	1923	—	—	—	—
17/9	10/2	12/9	7/8	Talsarnau ...	1004	1339	—	—	—	1653	1836	1916	—	—	—	—
17/3	10/-	12/3	7/6	Penrhyndeudraeth ...	1012	1348	—	—	—	1645	1829	1909	—	—	—	—
16/3	10/-	11/3	7/6	Portmadoc ...	1025	1358	—	—	—	1636	1807	1857	—	—	—	—
15/-	10/-	10/-	7/6	Criccieth ...	1038	1407	—	—	—	1626	1757	1848	—	—	—	—
15/-	10/-	10/-	7/6	Pwllheli ...	—		1020	1310	1430	—	—	—	1630	1708	1816	1908
Arrive Penychain Station for Holiday Camp					1047	1416	1028	1318	1439	—	—	—	—	—	—	—
Depart Penychain					—	—	—	—	—	1617	1748	1838	1621	1658	1807	1858

DETAILS OF OTHER TRAIN SERVICES ARE SHOWN ON PAGES 11 & 12

By booking the Combined Rail and Entrance Ticket, Day visitors to Butlin's Holiday Camp can save up to 2s. 6d. on each ticket purchased.

Holders of Holiday Runabout and "Family Week Out" Tickets, Area No. 16, may obtain Camp admission tickets at the reduced rate upon production of their tickets at their Booking Stations.

Butlin's Holiday Camp is open to visitors daily throughout the summer season between the hours of 10 a.m. and 6-30 p.m. (*Children must be accompanied by at least one adult to every three children*). Day visitors are entitled to use all the amenities including the Camp Restaurants and Coffee Bars. **All the licensed bars are open to Day Visitors.**

THE ENTERTAINMENTS AND AMUSEMENTS ARE FREE

You are given a free programme of entertainment on arrival and here are some of the many highlights available.

HEATED SWIMMING POOLS. Outdoors and Indoors

FREE AMUSEMENT PARK. With all kinds of free rides

SKATING RINK! PUTTING GREEN! BOATING LAKE! INDOOR GAMES ROOM! PLAYING FIELDS! DANCING! SHOWS! MANY NATIONAL COMPETITIONS! ALL SPORTS EQUIPMENT SUPPLIED FREE!

4

ABOVE LEFT AND ABOVE RIGHT: **The impact of the Butlin's camp on the railway and local economy must have been substantial. In terms of model operation, it is possible to have local trains, those specifically given over to Butlin's traffic, often travelling considerable distance, and excursions, land cruises and others of that ilk. Certainly, with residing holidaymakers and day visitors, the platforms at Penychain would have been heaving with passengers.**

RIGHT, BELOW LEFT AND BELOW RIGHT: **Penychain station** was originally opened on July 31, 1933, with a single track to Afon Wen, which was doubled in 1947 and switched back to single when Afon Wen closed. The building of a holiday camp began before the Second World War but was requisitioned for a naval training base, becoming Butlin's (Pwllheli) Camp in 1947. The station buildings on both platforms were of block construction with a second platform added and the original extended to accommodate ten coach trains. Both platforms were extra wide to accommodate the volume of holidaymakers. The station was not staffed in winter months. There was a 27-lever frame signal box, opened on March 31, 1947, with both lines signalled for two-way working. The accompanying photos are from July 30, 2023, and are fairly self-explanatory, although I particularly want to draw your attention to the terraced ramp, fencing and set of bypassing steps. This is where you waited with your suitcases for Butlin's 'Puffing Billy' road train to come and pick you up; the ramp ensured there were less people backing onto the platform and it made carrying wheel-less cases easier too.

ABOVE AND RIGHT: **Criccieth station** was a twin platform station within sight of the nearby castle. The main building is of brick construction, together with a brick and timber Dutton signal box with a 22 lever frame, stone goods shed (goods withdrawn from October 5, 1964) and two level crossings a little distance away. The black and white photos date from March 22, 1976, and the colour one from 1986.

Black Rock Halt on a curve near Graig Ddu, between Criccieth and Porthmadog, was comprised of a 100ft-long all-timber platform with no shelter. It opened on September 9, 1923, and closed on August 13, 1976.

RIGHT: **Wern Siding**, between Porthmadog and Criccieth, was used up to about 1964 in order to access stone. This section of track is quite steeply graded, and trains were often banked by steam locos from Porthmadog shed. An unidentified Class 25 with a solitary coal wagon, ventilated van, and brake van heads past the site of the siding towards Porthmadog. Old timetables are readily available secondhand and give a clear indication of freight operations.

SECTION G

BRITISH RAILWAYS
LONDON MIDLAND REGION
(WESTERN LINES)

WORKING TIME TABLE
OF
FREIGHT TRAINS
BETWEEN
CREWE AND HOLYHEAD
AND BRANCHES

9th SEPTEMBER 1963 to 14th JUNE 1964
(or until further notice)

When freight trains are running late, drivers must endeavour to make up time, with due regard to speed restrictions and the braking power of engine and train.

CREWE

J. ROYSTON
Line Manager

ABOVE AND OPPOSITE: **Porthmadog station** opened on October 10, 1867, and consists of two platforms with a brick and stone trimmed station building. The west signal box closed in 1932 and control passed to the east box with a 38-lever frame (originally 14 levers). This was a Dutton & Co. type 2, c1894, and closed in 1988. There was also a lattice footbridge, water columns, large water tank behind the main station building, a small goods shed, an extensive goods yard (freight still handled to 1973), sidings for coaches and a two-road loco shed. This was a sub-shed of Machynlleth and brick-built with a slate roof, which was re-covered in corrugated asbestos during the early 1950s. The shed closed in August 1963. The black and white photos are from March 22, 1976, with the colour ones taken on July 29, 2023.

THE STATION INN
The Pub on the Platform
FREE HOUSE
CASK ALES
CARLING
Worthingtons

SHOP

- Limited editions
- Exclusive products
- Modelling essentials

IN STOCK NOW! Laser-cut viaduct kits for 'OO' and 'TT:120' scales

New and exclusive to the Key Model World Shop are laser-cut kits to build this stunning model based on the Grade II listed Outwood Viaduct in Radcliffe, Manchester. The kits are available as an outer two arch kit and additional single arches to slot in between to extend the length. Full details online.

Prices: 'OO' outer two arch kit **£119.99** • 'OO' single arch kit **£47.99**
Prices: 'TT:120' outer two arch kit **£74.99** • 'TT:120' single arch kit **£29.99**

NEW! IN STOCK NOW

IN STOCK NOW! 'TT:120' laser-cut platform kits

Our latest release for 'TT:120' scale is a pair of platform kits based on those featuring in our 'TT:120' layout build series. Option A makes a 1,115mm long, 60mm wide platform with a 156mm wide section to accommodate Hornby's Skaledale 'TT:120' station – TT9002. Option B makes a 950mm long, 60mm wide platform with a 100mm wide section to accommodate the Skaledale 'TT:120' waiting room - TT9003.

IN STOCK NOW! Great Northern Railway Tunnel Portals

New and available now are our laser-cut kits for a double track tunnel portal based on the Great Northern Railway design at Hadley Wood. The kits are available for 'OO' and 'TT:120 scales.

Prices: 'OO' Gauge **£54.99** **Prices:** 'TT:120' **£29.99**

WE ARE AN OFFICIAL HORNBY TT:120 STOCKIST!

Shop the full Hornby TT:120 range on the Key Model World Shop including locomotives, carriages, wagons, track and accessories as well as buildings.

modelling products or visit...

orld.com/shop

Minffordd to Morfa Mawddach

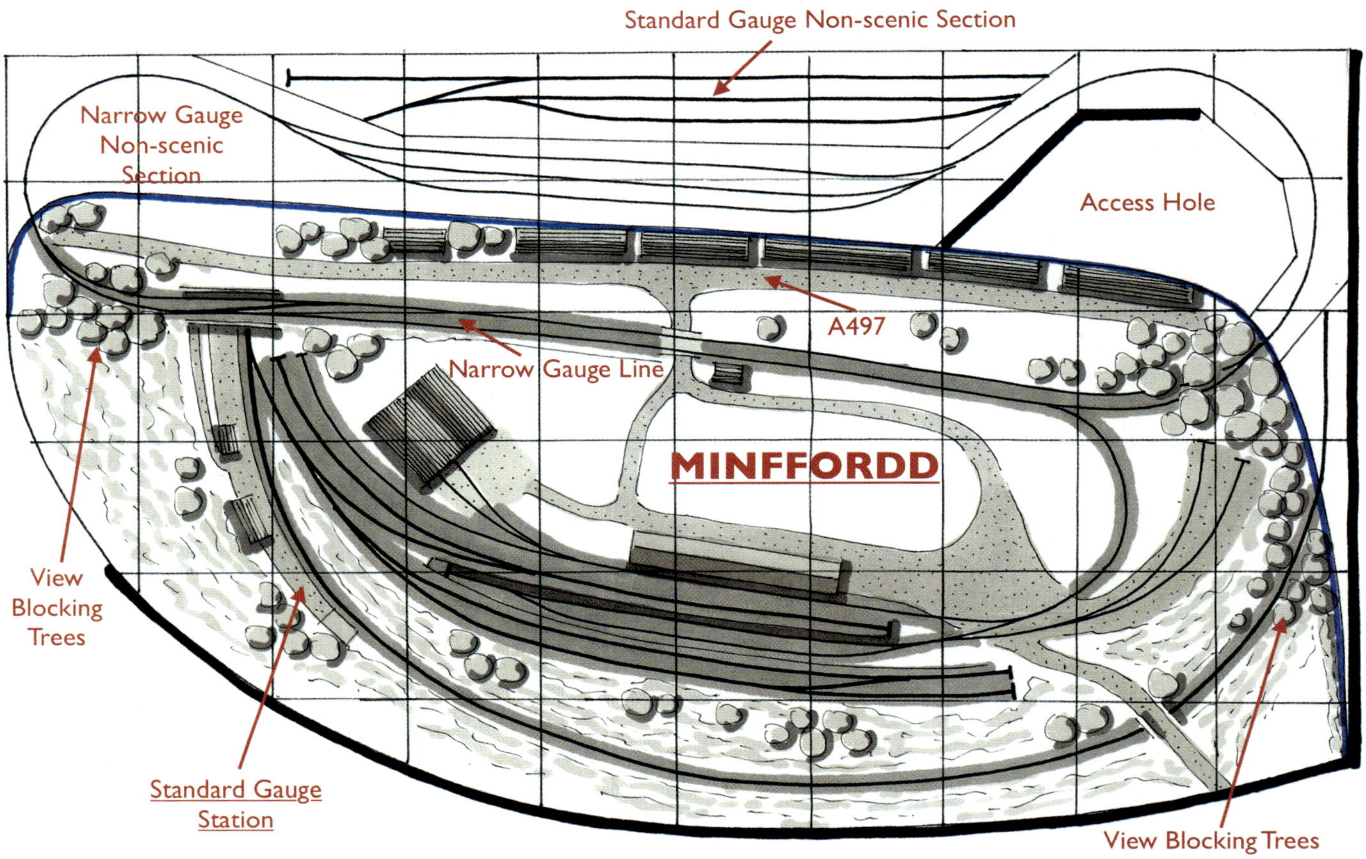

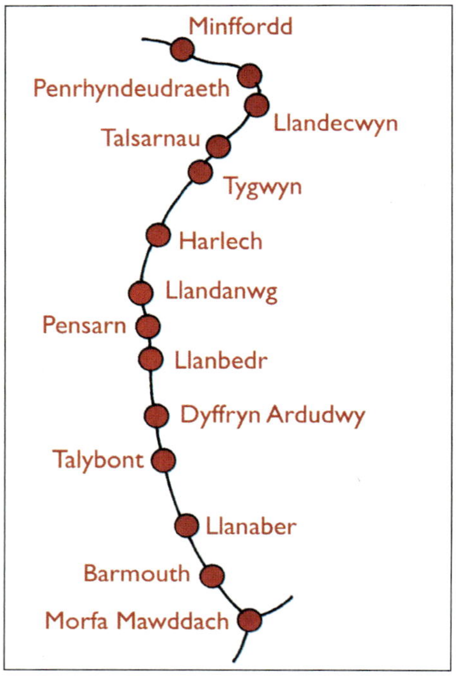

History and description at a glance

If you are interested in standard and narrow gauge together, then Minffordd is the perfect place. As a designer, the difficult bit is how you tie up route ends and have sufficient space for two fiddle yards at different levels. This OO/OO9 layout measures 10ft by 6ft and requires a room 14ft by 10ft, giving minimum access of 2ft all the way round. The narrow gauge loop, between two standard gauge sidings, is lower to allow for the transfer of material, whereas the narrow gauge line and adjacent sidings, feeding Maenofferen Slate Quarry shed, are higher than the adjacent standard gauge line.

Location by location

Minffordd station is on a snaking, graded route, requiring banking in steam days. Surrounded by trees in the modern photos

taken on July 26, 2023, it was very much in open ground at the time of the earlier photo on March 22, 1976, with the remnants of a 19-lever frame, brick, and timber signal box. The station is situated below the narrow gauge line, with a footpath and small underpass linking the two. There were standard gauge sidings into an interchange with the narrow gauge line and slate was transferred here to 1946, when it passed to road transport. One of the last trains to enter the yard was in May 1972.

Penrhyndeudraeth station is a single platform station with a typical Cambrian brick-built building and platform-mounted, 18-lever signal box. There were cattle pens, dock, a goods shed and a crossing keeper's house. It is an unusual trackplan for the line in having two loops, consisting of three tracks, for almost the full length of the site. The nearby Briwet Bridge, for both rail and road traffic, was wooden trestle at the time but is now a concrete structure. The 14.11.DMU to Pwllheli heads away from the camera with Cooke's factory spreading out over the hillside behind, both photo taken on March 22, 1976. The station, factory and bridge would make an interesting oval-shaped layout. In the accompanying OO gauge 12ft by 7ft plan, I have included all the salient features, although not without radical compression and some manipulation of track, especially at the left hand end, and which is almost all Setrack.

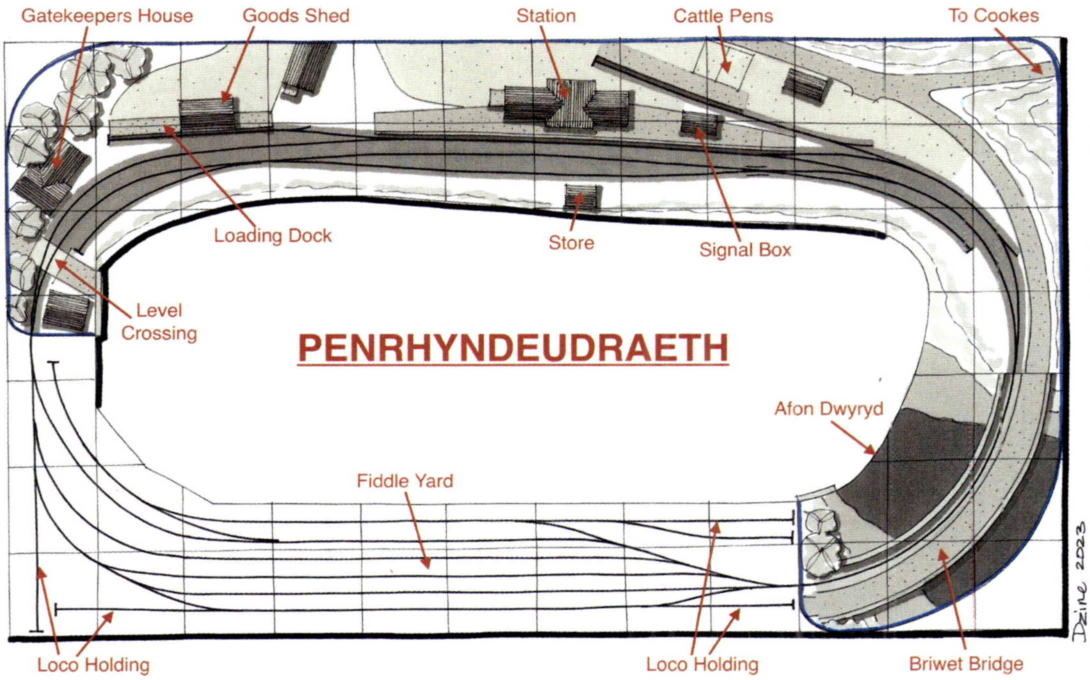

LEFT: **82000 departs Penrhyndeudraeth for Pwllheli on August 26. 1964. Note the distant level crossing and nearby keeper's house.** Richard Inwood/ Paul A Lunn Collection

conveyed, and his own name and address, and also the name and address of the proposed consignee, and has had an intimation from the Commission that they are prepared to receive such consignment.

3 Consignments of Explosives (other than Class 6 Division 1 Explosives consigned for carriage by passenger train) shall be sent to the Commission's forwarding station, and shall be received by their servants, only at such times during the hours of daylight, that is to say between sunrise and sunset, as the Commission may by notice appoint, and every consignment and package containing any Explosive proposed to be conveyed on the railway other than by passenger train shall immediately on the arrival thereof at the Commission's station or wharf on the railway be delivered to and be received by the Commission's servants authorised to receive dangerous goods, and by no other person whatsoever.

4 No Explosive (other than Class 6 Division 1 Explosives consigned for carriage by passenger train) shall be loaded or unloaded on the Commission's premises by the consignor or consignee thereof, or the Commission's servants, except between sunrise and sunset.

5 No Explosive other than Class 6 Division 1 Explosives shall be conveyed by passenger train on the railway.

6 Gunpowder and any Explosive authorised by the Secretary of State to be packed in metallic cases or cylinders as outer packages, if packed in metallic cases or cylinders which fulfil all the requirements of the Explosives Act, 1875, and are of a pattern approved by the Commission, may be conveyed along with ordinary goods traffic in a carriage not containing any article or substance liable to cause or communicate fire or explosion.

7 No Explosive of the 5th (Fulminate) class, nor any Explosive of the 6th (Ammunition) class containing its own means of ignition, nor any Explosive of the 7th (Firework) class, shall be conveyed in the same carriage with any Explosive not of the class and division to which it belongs.

8 There shall not be conveyed in the same carriage with any Explosive (other than any of the Class 6 Division 1 Explosives in the course of carriage by passenger train) anything of the nature of lucifer or other matches, acids or other chemicals, petroleum or

3

other inflammable liquid, calcium carbide, oily goods, charcoal, lamp black, or any other article or substance of an inflammable nature or liable to spontaneous ignition or to cause or communicate fire or explosion.

9 On each side of every carriage containing any Explosive (other than any of the Class 6 Division 1 Explosives in the course of carriage by passenger train) there shall be fixed in conspicuous characters, by means of a securely attached label or otherwise, the word 'Explosive' or the name of the Explosive with the word 'Explosive', except when containing Explosive packed in metallic cases or cylinders as provided for in the sixth of these bye-laws, and every carriage containing Explosive (other than any of the Class 6 Division 1 Explosives in the course of carriage by passenger train) shall be placed as far as practicable in the middle of the train.

10 Not more than five carriages containing Explosive shall be loaded or unloaded at or on any railway station or wharf on the railway or be attached to or conveyed by any one train at any one time, and the quantity of Explosive to be contained or loaded in any one such carriage at any one time shall not exceed 16,000 lb. in weight, provided always that the quantity of Explosive to be contained or loaded in any one such carriage shall not exceed one ton in weight, unless the carriage shall be a covered van.

11 Explosive contained in metallic cases or cylinders, if conveyed in open trucks, shall be sheeted so as effectually to protect it against communication of fire.

12 Explosive (other than Class 6 Division 1 Explosives and such Explosives of the 2nd Division of the 7th (Firework) class as are defined as 'Shop Goods' by Order in Council No. 16A of the 11th May, 1906), shall, unless contained in metallic cases or cylinders, be conveyed only in a gunpowder van.

13 When the stowing of Explosive in any carriage or the loading or unloading of any Explosive is undertaken by any person other than the Commission, all due precautions shall be taken by such person, by careful stowing and loading and unloading and otherwise, to prevent and secure such Explosive from being brought into contact with or endangered by any other article or substance liable to cause fire or explosion.

4

14 In loading or unloading any Explosive, the packages containing the same shall, as far as practicable, be passed from hand to hand, and not be rolled upon the ground, and in no case shall any such packages be rolled, unless clean hides, cloths, or sheets have been previously laid down on the platform or ground over which the same are to be rolled. Packages containing Explosive shall not be thrown or dropped down, but shall be carefully deposited and stowed in such manner as to prevent any displacement of the packages during transit.

15 No person, while employed in loading, stowing in any carriage, or unloading any Explosive,

(a) shall smoke or have about his person any lucifer match, explosive or means of striking a light;

(b) shall, save while loading, stowing or unloading Class 6 Division 1 Explosives or such Explosives of the 2nd Division of the 7th (Firework) class as are defined as 'Shop Goods' by Order in Council No. 16A of the 11th May, 1906, wear boots or shoes with steel or iron nails, steel or iron heels, or metal tips of any kind.

16 While the loading, unloading or conveyance of Explosive is going on, all persons engaged in such loading, unloading, or conveyance shall observe all due precautions for the prevention of accidents by fire or explosion and for preventing unauthorised persons having access to the Explosive so being loaded, unloaded, or conveyed, and shall abstain from any act whatever which tends to cause fire or explosion, and is not reasonably necessary for the purpose of loading, unloading, or conveyance of such Explosive, or of any other article carried therewith, and for preventing any other person from committing any such act: and such other person who, after being warned, commits any such act shall be deemed to commit a breach of this bye-law.

17 The loading or unloading of Explosive into or out of any carriage when once begun, shall be proceeded with with all due diligence until the same is completed.

18 Packages containing any Explosive must be removed by the consignee from the station, wharf or depot of the Commission to which they have been conveyed, as soon as practicable and with all due diligence after arrival; and such packages shall in the

5

ABOVE AND LEFT: **Cooke's explosives factory dates back to 1865. Cooke bought it from the Ministry of Munitions in 1922 and sold it to ICI in 1958. Work ceased in 1995 and the site was cleared by 1999. The cattle dock siding was used for loading explosives, an important source of traffic, until transferred to the Ffestiniog line. There is an excellent British Film Institute silent colour film at www.player.bfi.org.uk. It shows the works in detail and the firm's maroon-liveried lorries travelling down to the station, followed by some of the process of loading in the last frames. The accompanying rule book extracts give much useful information to modellers in terms of trains and handling explosives.**

RIGHT: **Landecwyn Halt** opened on November 18, 1935, and had a 75ft long timber trestle platform with pent corrugated shelter, typical of others found along the line. It was in a stunning riverside setting with Cooke's Works distant centre left and would make the perfect extension to the Penrhyndeudraeth trackplan in a 16ft by 8ft garage. The photo was taken on March 22, 1976.

LEFT: **Talsarnau station** featured buildings constructed from local stone, with a brick plinth and timber signal box containing 11 levers. There were two sidings, with one used for a camping coach during the course of its life. Note the distant mountain range seen on March 22, 1976.

ABOVE AND RIGHT: **Ty Gwyn Halt** opened on July 11, 1927, and featured a timber-faced platform that was 71ft long with a corrugated pent shelter. Again, seen on March 22, 1976.

Harlech station

LEFT: Apart from a second level crossing, behind the camera, and castle high on the hill to my right, you can see all the various components of the station site. This included a GWR type 8a signal box with 29 lever frame, which opened in 1924 and closed on October 23, 1988, along with a footbridge and provender store. Livestock and agriculture figured highly at Harlech, when recorded on March 22, 1976. I have been unable to find the exact date, but there was no footbridge in 1953 and one had been built by 1963, possibly tied into a royal event? The castle at Harlech is much nearer the station than that at Criccieth in terms of distance though probably not in height. If you are a modeller with additional interests and castles are your thing, this location would be a great place to start.

ABOVE: Provender stores provided instant goods storage. They were made from pre-fabricated sectional reinforced concrete panels, mounted on piles (legs) to prevent dampness and rodents eating agricultural supplies. This example at Harlech, see in 1986, replaced some old, grounded coach bodies.

ABOVE: Llandanwg Halt, opened on November 18, 1929, had a 75ft long timber-faced platform with a corrugated pent waiting shelter, accessed by a sloping path from the nearby brick road bridge. Without any previous warning, I was lucky to catch this rare works train late in the evening on March 22, 1976, hence the lack of quality.

LEFT: **Llanbedr and Pensarn station (now Pensarn)** consists of a single platform on a gentle curve, with a brick-built station building. There was a platform-mounted 34-lever signal box about halfway down the platform and dating from the 1930s, having replaced a Cambrian-built box located by the hand-operated level crossing. Additionally, there was a cattle dock and yard with a small warehouse (removed by 1948) between the goods line and down loop. It is possible that parts and equipment were delivered here for the airfield at Llanbedr and would justify greater modelling intensity around the time of the Second World War.

RIGHT: **Talwrn Bach Halt** (now named Llanbedr) is seen on March 22, 1976. The accompanying photo shows why we should never rush to put our track down on a flat topped baseboard. The lowest ground level, at the bottom of the embankment, is where the baseboard needs to be and then built upwards to track level. In this way, the line will look more as if it has passed through the landscape and, more importantly, when we take low-level photos, the baseboard edge will not be visible. This was originally a timber trestle platform, later replaced with a 100ft long pre-cast concrete one, and served the nearby Royal Aircraft Establishment at Llanbedr Airfield. During 1940/41, there would have been Spitfires and then USAAF Lightnings and much more for those with an interest in model aircraft. I have found no evidence of any rail served connection, though there are some interesting groundworks shown on Google Maps, nearby!

LEFT: **Dyffryn Ardudwy station** had a brick built station building with a 13 lever frame signal box, constructed from timber and corrugated sheet over a brick base, on the up platform. There was a small goods yard with two sidings (goods traffic withdrawn December 2, 1963), a store, cattle pen, loading dock, small shed, weighbridge and office, and a level crossing at the south end. Seen on March 22, 1976.

RIGHT: **Tal-y-Bont Halt** framed within the nearby Ffordd Glan-Mor bridge. The platform face is from redundant sleepers, back-filled and covered with chippings and had a corrugated shelter with elliptical roof. Seen on March 22, 1976, this was fairly unique in that both the access path and track share the same bridge span.

Llanaber Halt opened in 1911 had a 202ft long platform with a gable-ended wooden shelter, wood post and rail fence, and served nearby caravan sites. There is a footbridge south of the halt.

Over the Years: Barmouth station

ABOVE: **82000 on its way to Pwllheli on August 26, 1964. In the distance is Barmouth North signal box with a 36 lever frame.** This closed in **July 1975, having been replaced by a ground frame.**
Richard Inwood/Paul A Lunn Collection

ABOVE: **There is much to be seen in this photo, including a rarely-modelled footbridge landing sited on top of a building. The bay/excursion platform to the right of the shot was used for the Dolgellau shuttle and for stabling steam locos; its use ended in1975). The South signal box dated from 1890 and had 27 levers at this time, up from the original 15.**

ABOVE: **This original Cambrian ticket office, seen in 1986, probably served the bay/excursion platform and was subsequently preserved. You can just see the South signal box behind. It appears on a plan on page 13, at the corner of Jubilee and Beach Road, in *An Historical Survey of Selected Great Western Stations* by R.H. Clark (ISBN 0 86093 015 7).**

ABOVE AND BELOW: **Barmouth South box was a Dutton & Co. Type 1 with a 27-lever frame and principally worked the level crossing.**

ABOVE: **The main station building at Barmouth opened on June 3, 1867, and is situated between the town and beach. There are extra-long platforms to cope with holiday traffic.**

RIGHT: **Apart from modern signage, all elevations remain largely unchanged. As a single storey building, surveying for modelmaking purpose should be relatively easy.**

Between Barmouth Station and Bridge

LEFT: **This section of track, near the quay, is one of my favourites. I just love the way 80104 squeezes between two slate cottages, past what was once an engineer's site to the right, on August 29, 1964.** Richard Inwood/Paul A Lunn Collection

Over the years

ABOVE: **An unidentified Class 24 (5011, 5085 and 5092 would all be suitable modelling examples) is Pwllheli-bound with three coal wagons, a low-height gunpowder van, a ventilated van, and a brake. I particularly want to draw your attention to the hill, Garn Gorllwyn, on the right and how little vegetation exists, even by early September. Taken September 4, 1964.**

ABOVE: **I love this 'modern', simple concrete block and span bridge, near Porkington Terrace, on March 22, 1976. Again, I want to draw your attention the lack of vegetation on the sharply rising rocky outcrop behind, it is minimal as you would expect for March.**

ABOVE: **Here is the last of three photos in this series, designed to show how vegetation varies over seasons and years. By the time of my visit on July 29, 2023, it has got quite a foothold.**

LEFT AND ABOVE: **Before Barmouth Bridge, there is a sharp, check-railed curve which passes under a tunnel-like bridge, seen in more detail in the accompanying close up on July 29, 2023. It is the perfect corner for a layout to mask a non-scenic fiddle yard. The varied levels from embankments, path, road, houses, and rocky outcrop make for a pleasing composition. 7816 is seen on a Machynlleth-bound train on August 26, 1964.** Richard Inwood/Paul A Lunn Collection

Back in time

ABOVE AND RIGHT: **The north end approach to Barmouth Bridge, shown in both photos but almost 60 years apart, with little scenic change. The only major difference is the traction with 7816 on August 26, 1964, and a Class 158 on July 29, 2023.** Richard Inwood/Paul A Lunn Collection

RIGHT: **Opened for traffic in 1867, Barmouth Bridge carries the line over the Mawddach Estuary. Rebuilt between 1906 and 1909, the bridge thereafter consisted of four metal spans; two straight and two bow string girder, all of lattice construction, of which one was an opening section, requiring a team of eight men to turn. This section has rarely been opened in recent times, though shown here on a pre-1923 postcard, when tall ships were still in use. It was last opened for testing in the 1980s and will no longer open after the 2023 rebuild.**

LEFT: **Right up to date and the metal spans are about to be replaced in July 2023, hence new vertical beams on top of the bow girders as part of a construction to carry an overhead crane.**

BELOW LEFT AND BELOW RIGHT: **An unmistakably attractive structure, the bridge has featured on many images, particularly when more recent steam-operated specials have traversed the line, in this case during the summer of 1987.**

BRITISH RAILWAYS

NEW FOR 1987 .....

THE CARDIGAN BAY EXPRESS

Steam on the Cambrian Coast Line
Machynlleth to Barmouth, Aberystwyth and Pwllheli

SUMMER 1987

Rheilffordd y Cambrian
Cambrian Coast Line

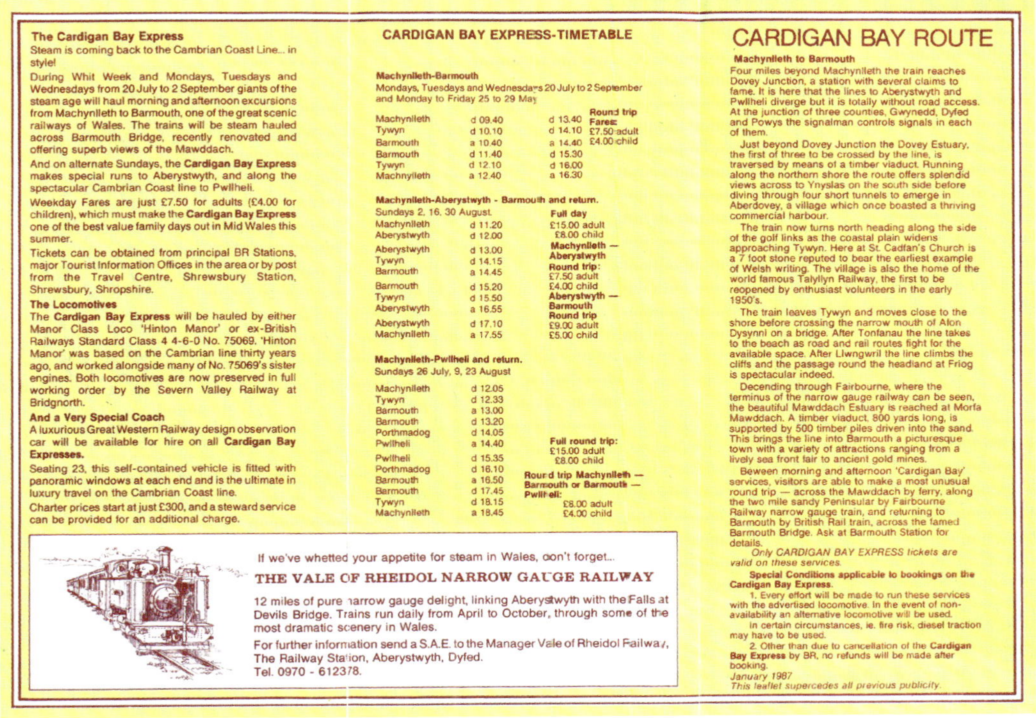

The Cardigan Bay Express

Steam is coming back to the Cambrian Coast Line... in style!

During Whit Week and Mondays, Tuesdays and Wednesdays from 20 July to 2 September giants of the steam age will haul morning and afternoon excursions from Machynlleth to Barmouth, one of the great scenic railways of Wales. The trains will be steam hauled across Barmouth Bridge, recently renovated and offering superb views of the Mawddach.

And on alternate Sundays, the **Cardigan Bay Express** makes special runs to Aberystwyth, and along the spectacular Cambrian Coast line to Pwllheli.

Weekday Fares are just £7.50 for adults (£4.00 for children), which must make the **Cardigan Bay Express** one of the best value family days out in Mid Wales this summer.

Tickets can be obtained from principal BR Stations, major Tourist Information Offices in the area or by post from the Travel Centre, Shrewsbury Station, Shrewsbury, Shropshire.

The Locomotives

The **Cardigan Bay Express** will be hauled by either Manor Class Loco 'Hinton Manor' or ex-British Railways Standard Class 4 4-6-0 No. 75069. 'Hinton Manor' was based on the Cambrian line thirty years ago, and worked alongside many of No. 75069's sister engines. Both locomotives are now preserved in full working order by the Severn Valley Railway at Bridgnorth.

And a Very Special Coach

A luxurious Great Western Railway design observation car will be available for hire on all **Cardigan Bay Expresses.**

Seating 23, this self-contained vehicle is fitted with panoramic windows at each end and is the ultimate in luxury travel on the Cambrian Coast line.

Charter prices start at just £300, and a steward service can be provided for an additional charge.

CARDIGAN BAY EXPRESS-TIMETABLE

Machynlleth-Barmouth

Mondays, Tuesdays and Wednesdays 20 July to 2 September and Monday to Friday 25 to 29 May

Machynlleth	d 09.40	d 13.40	**Round trip Fares:**
Tywyn	d 10.10	d 14.10	£7.50 adult
Barmouth	a 10.40	a 14.40	£4.00 child
Barmouth	d 11.40	d 15.30	
Tywyn	d 12.10	d 16.00	
Machnylleth	a 12.40	a 16.30	

Machynlleth-Aberystwyth - Barmouth and return.

Sundays 2, 16, 30 August.

Machynlleth	d 11.20	**Full day** £15.00 adult
Aberystwyth	d 12.00	£8.00 child
Aberystwyth	d 13.00	**Machynlleth — Aberystwyth**
Tywyn	d 14.15	**Round trip:**
Barmouth	a 14.45	£7.50 adult
Barmouth	d 15.20	£4.00 child
Tywyn	d 15.50	**Aberystwyth — Barmouth**
Aberystwyth	a 16.55	**Round trip**
Aberystwyth	d 17.10	£9.00 adult
Machynlleth	a 17.55	£5.00 child

Machynlleth-Pwllheli and return.

Sundays 26 July, 9, 23 August

Machynlleth	d 12.05	
Tywyn	d 12.33	
Barmouth	a 13.00	
Barmouth	d 13.20	
Porthmadog	d 14.05	
Pwllheli	a 14.40	**Full round trip:**
Pwllheli	d 15.35	£15.00 adult £8.00 child
Porthmadog	d 16.10	**Round trip Machynlleth —**
Barmouth	a 16.50	**Barmouth or Barmouth —**
Barmouth	d 17.45	**Pwllheli:**
Tywyn	d 18.15	£8.00 adult
Machynlleth	a 18.45	£4.00 child

If we've whetted your appetite for steam in Wales, don't forget...

THE VALE OF RHEIDOL NARROW GAUGE RAILWAY

12 miles of pure narrow gauge delight, linking Aberystwyth with the Falls at Devils Bridge. Trains run daily from April to October, through some of the most dramatic scenery in Wales.

For further information send a S.A.E. to the Manager Vale of Rheidol Railway, The Railway Station, Aberystwyth, Dyfed.
Tel. 0970 - 612378.

CARDIGAN BAY ROUTE

Machynlleth to Barmouth

Four miles beyond Machynlleth the train reaches Dovey Junction, a station with several claims to fame. It is here that the lines to Aberystwyth and Pwllheli diverge but it is totally without road access. At the junction of three counties, Gwynedd, Dyfed and Powys the signalman controls signals in each of them.

Just beyond Dovey Junction the Dovey Estuary, the first of three to be crossed by the line, is traversed by means of a timber viaduct. Running along the northern shore the route offers splendid views across to Ynyslas on the south side before diving through four short tunnels to emerge in Aberdovey, a village which once boasted a thriving commercial harbour.

The train now turns north heading along the side of the golf links as the coastal plain widens approaching Tywyn. Here at St. Cadfan's Church is a 7 foot stone reputed to bear the earliest example of Welsh writing. The village is also the home of the world famous Talyllyn Railway, the first to be reopened by enthusiast volunteers in the early 1950's.

The train leaves Tywyn and moves close to the shore before crossing the narrow mouth of Afon Dysynni on a bridge. After Tonfanau the line takes to the beach as road and rail routes fight for the available space. After Llwngwril the line climbs the cliffs and the passage round the headland at Friog is spectacular indeed.

Decending through Fairbourne, where the terminus of the narrow gauge railway can be seen, the beautiful Mawddach Estuary is reached at Morfa Mawddach. A timber viaduct, 800 yards long, is supported by 500 timber piles driven into the sand. This brings the line into Barmouth a picturesque town with a variety of attractions ranging from a lively sea front fair to ancient gold mines.

Beween morning and afternoon 'Cardigan Bay' services, visitors are able to make a most unusual round trip — across the Mawddach by ferry, along the two mile sandy Peninsular by Fairbourne Railway narrow gauge train, and returning to Barmouth by British Rail train, across the famed Barmouth Bridge. Ask at Barmouth Station for details.

Only CARDIGAN BAY EXPRESS tickets are valid on these services.

Special Conditions applicable to bookings on the Cardigan Bay Express.

1. Every effort will be made to run these services with the advertised locomotive. In the event of non-availability an alternative locomotive will be used.

In certain circumstances, ie. fire risk, diesel traction may have to be used.

2. Other than due to cancellation of the **Cardigan Bay Express** by BR, no refunds will be made after booking.

January 1987
This leaflet supercedes all previous publicity.

ABOVE: **It is only when you get really close up that you realise the poor state of the 156-year old steel sections and that the 2023 project to remove and replace them was an absolute necessity.**

In the detail

A much reduced length O gauge scale model of Barmouth Bridge exists at the Fairbourne Miniature Railway and although it is nothing like the length of the real version, it works well enough for me. In OO gauge, I think you could get it down to about 12ft in total, 5ft for the metalwork and 7ft for the wooden trestles, though I suppose the obvious solution, if you are looking for a wow factor, would be to reduce to TT or N. With smaller scales, you can have the benefit of proportional reduction or conversely make a slightly longer and therefore more impressive model.

ABOVE LEFT, MIDDLE AND RIGHT: **Often referred to as an 'A' frame, I include these close up photos of the Baltic timber fames and deck to aid model construction. In reality, they have suffered from marine worm infection and as a result, the bridge was closed from October 13, 1980, to May 22, 1981, for repairs. During that time, separate DMUs ran from Pwllheli to Barmouth, and a connecting bus service was provided to maintain the link with the rest of the line.**

Unusual and rarely modelled

Every once in a while, something spectacular comes along, a scenic eyecatcher quite like no other. With the original girder spans deteriorating badly, it was only a matter of time before action would be needed. A solution to replace all the girder sections commenced and a base was set up near Morfa Mawwdach station to test bed the process. My understanding is that a box section girder (grey) will be mounted on six low-level flatbed wagons and two new bow girders (black) strapped to the side. The first experiment just to get the whole thing mounted is imminent as I write. If successful, during a three month line closure, the whole construction, in separate parts, will be craned onto the line; first the wagons, then box girder followed by the bow spans. It will then be pushed, using an onsite Unimog road-rail vehicle, onto the existing 1867 supporting columns. As the new spans are nearer together, at this time, they will fit inside the old ones. Once in position, the old bridge spans will be cut into small sections and dropped onto pontoons waiting at water level. At this point, the new spans will be craned into the positions of the old ones, deck and braces added, no doubt using the temporary overhead moving crane. Although most, if not all, of the opening equipment will be retained for visual authenticity, the bridge will no longer open. Apart from a great feat of engineering, the test bed site would be a relatively easy one to model.

ABOVE: **82005 at Morfa Mawddach with a Pwllheli to Machynlleth train on August 26, 1964. You can just see the roof of the 38-lever frame signal box behind the third coach.** Richard Inwood/Paul A Lunn Collection

LEFT AND BELOW: **All that was left on March 23, 1976, after demolition, a sad state after its former glory. The station was named Barmouth Junction until June 13, 1960, when it changed to Morfa Mawddach.**

ABOVE: **The all timber box footprint measured 31ft by 10ft. There were up to three camping coaches at the station. The line, right foreground, is that to Dolgellau, which closed in 1965.**

RIGHT: **Although now revitalised, the very basic station is exceptionally busy with bikers and walkers and the odd railway enthusiast! Odd meaning occasional, of course not odd as in...you know what I mean.**

Fairbourne to Gogarth Halt

Real inspiration, fictitious interpretation

ABOVE AND BELOW: **This pair of mainly fictitious N gauge layouts in a space of approximately 5ft by 3ft show there is more than one interpretation to a design; it all depends on what you want to prioritise. The first has a larger scenic area and slightly more remote feel about it, whereas the second has a larger fiddle yard. Both have stations inspired by Fairbourne, an explosives siding from Maentwrog Road, and a short wooden trestle bridge based on that near Dovey Junction.**

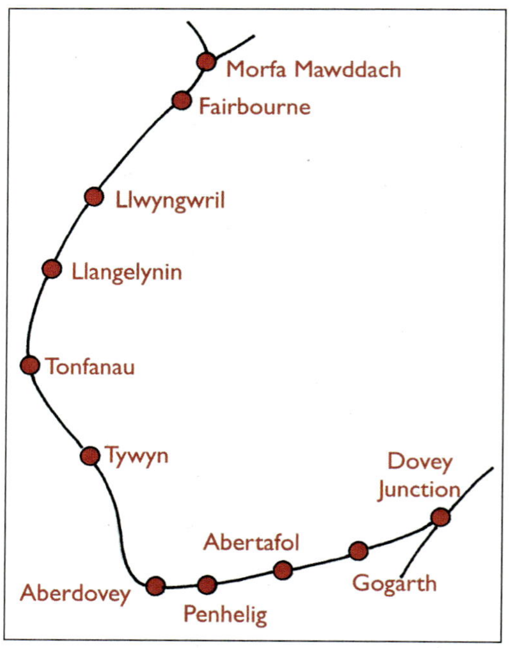

Location by location

LEFT AND FAR LEFT: **Fairbourne station opened on May 6, 1899, and in later years there was a solitary siding, mainly used for a camping coach. I do not recall anyone modelling staff adding a signal lamp, especially up the ladder. Also note the ground frame in close proximity to the level crossing gate, as seen on September 1, 1975.**

ABOVE LEFT, ABOVE RIGHT, LEFT AND BELOW: **Modern day Fairbourne, which serves as an interchange for the miniature railway, is much changed these days, although I was fascinated by the activity in the old yard. The TXM Plant wagon is the same type as those involved in the Barmouth Bridge reconstruction and I suspect was surplus to requirements., as seen on July 31, 2023.**

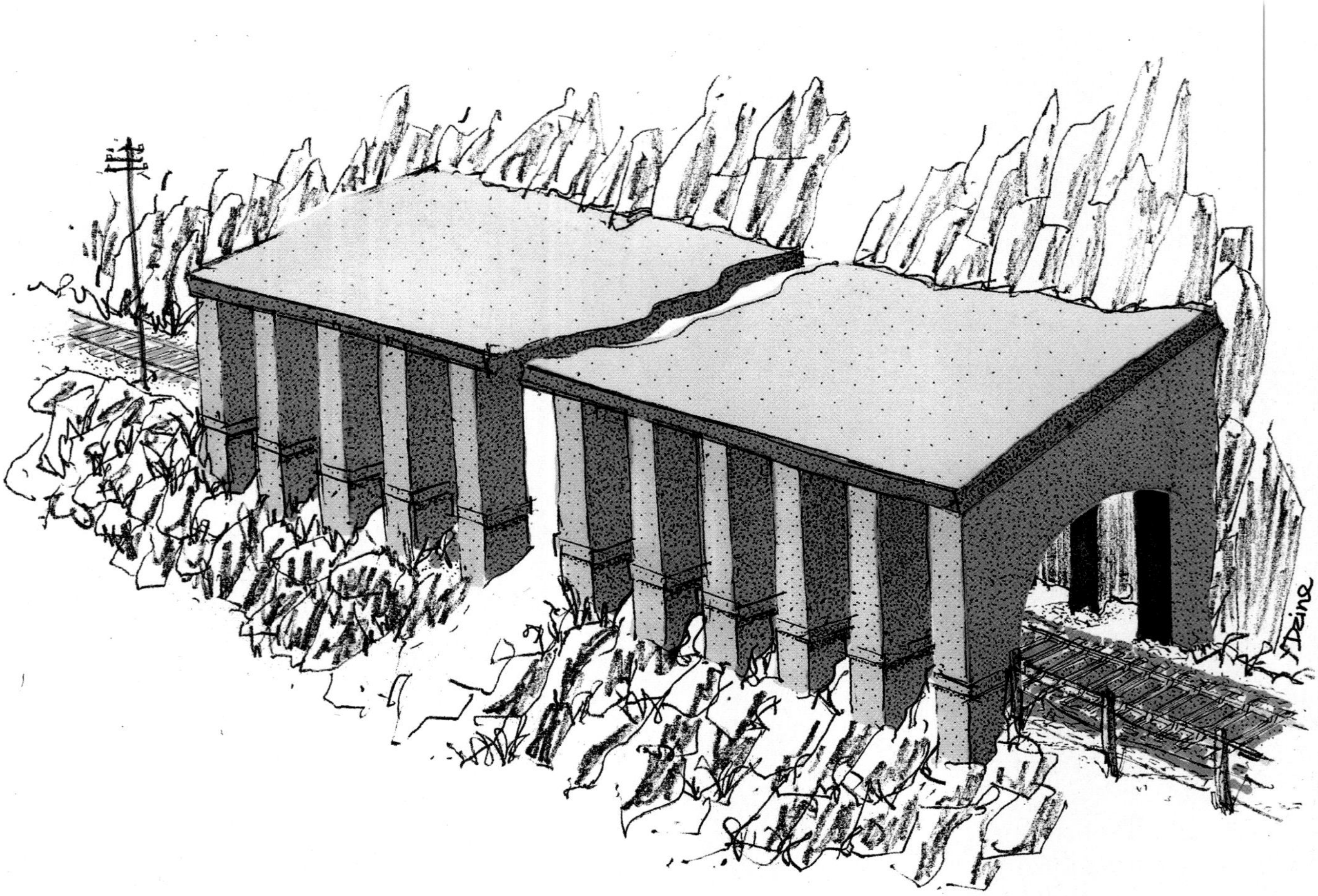

ABOVE AND BELOW: **Friog** is at the high point of a steep gradient, varying between 1:76 to 1:55, from Fairbourne, and on reaching the rock shelter, is approximately 100ft above sea level. As a result of major landslides on January 01, 1883, and March 4, 1933, a shelter was built, this measuring 60 yards long and with a 1ft thick reinforced concrete pitched roof and heavily reinforced arches. An adjacent area was also strengthened with masonry and tied with old rails. Further reinforcement was undertaken in the late 1970s and scaffolding was erected over the line at the northern end and down to the sea; a particularly unusual and rarely modelled feature. A model of the shelter could be customised to any length rather than the real life 60 yards, which equates to 2ft 5in in OO gauge or 1ft 2½in for N.

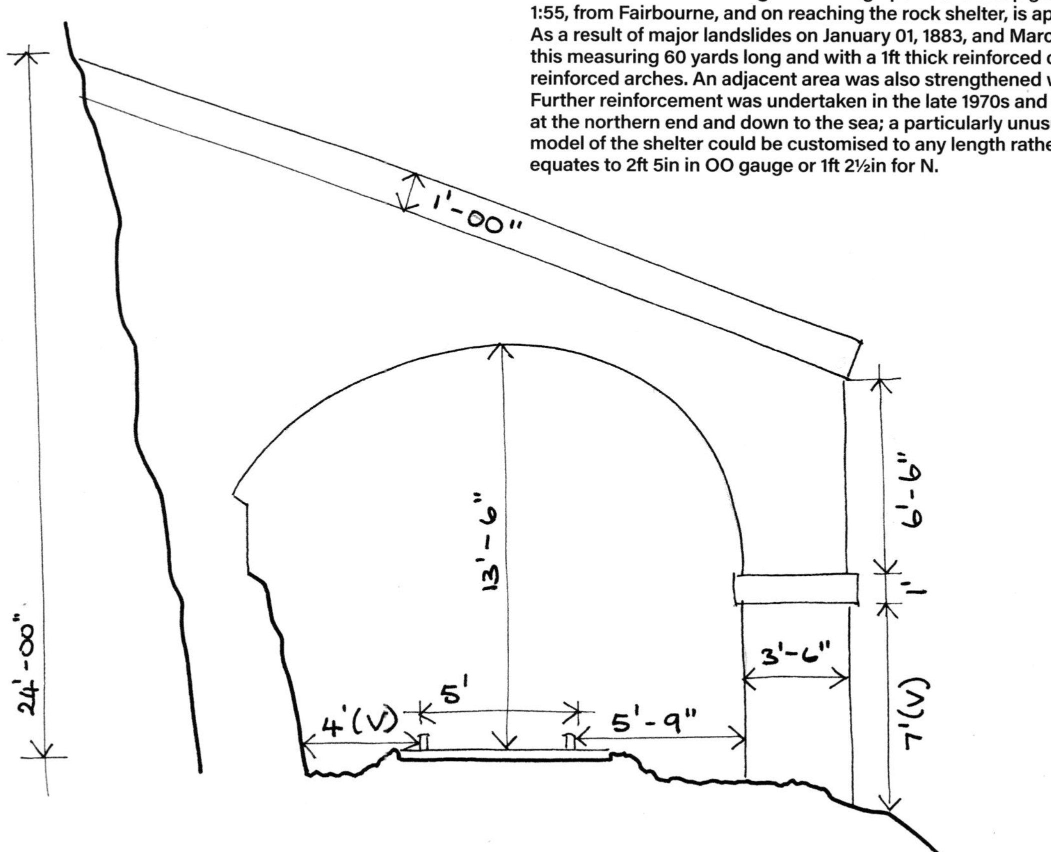

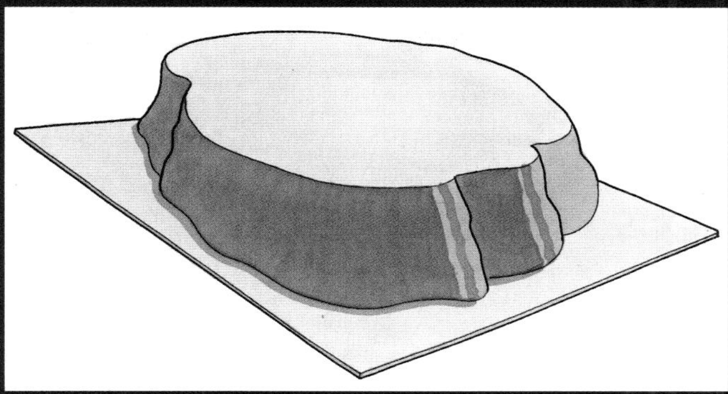

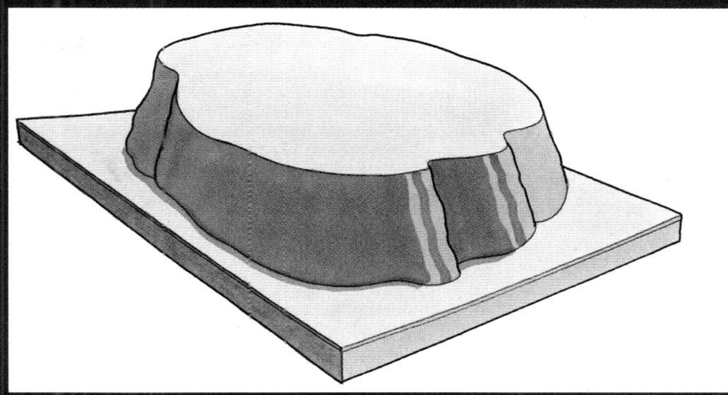

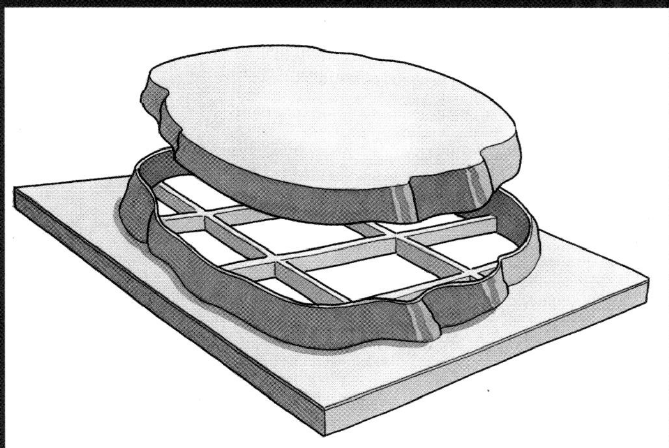

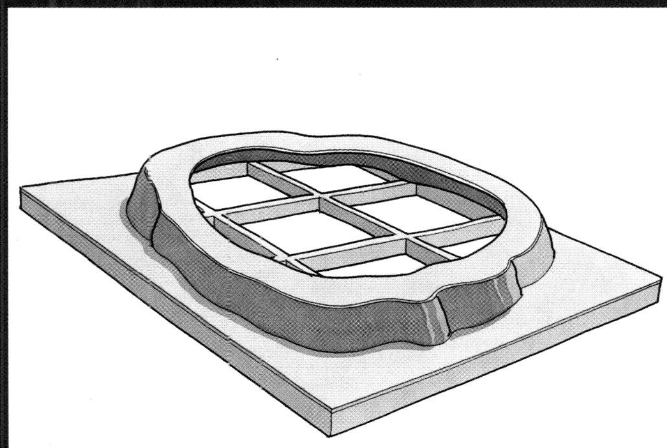

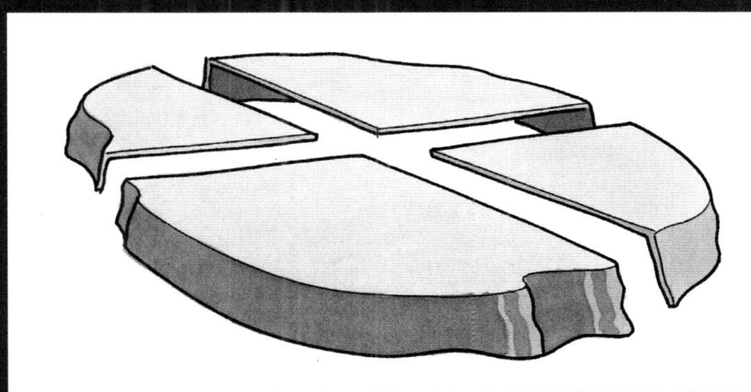

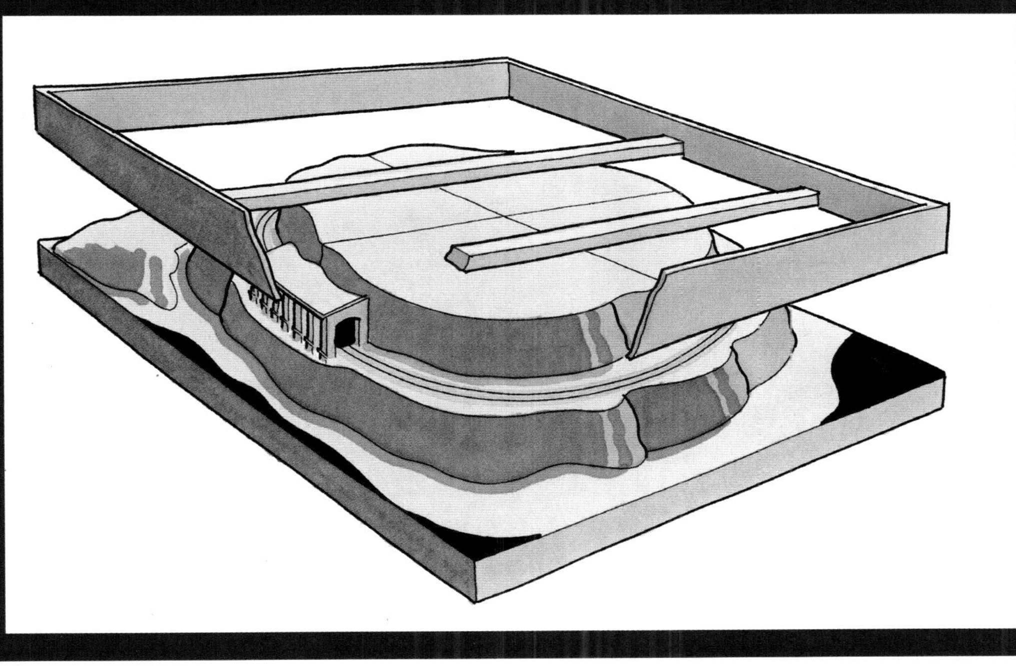

This N gauge layout design is an idea by good friend and modeller Paul Marshall-Potter. It uses an upturned pond liner, cut as shown, to create a ridge unit for plain track, possibly with a loop or sidings to the rear and Friog Shelter as one of the main scenic components. You could add storage inside the main hill, accessed by removing the upper fascia board and frame.

Llwyngwril station has un-equal length platforms with brick, rendered walls and slate station building. There was a large water tank, a single siding sometimes used for a camping coach, and a 13 -lever Cambrian Railway signal box with an overhanging end section. Goods facilities were withdrawn on May 4, 1964.

LEFT: **Llangelynin Halt** opened on July 7, 1930. It had a stockade-type wood-faced curving platform with a corrugated pent roof shelter, two short lamp-mounted posts and the accompanying dishevelled sign, some distance away and closer to the road.

ABOVE: **Ton Fanau station** is one of my favourites, with multiple structures on a stone-faced platform, as seen on September 1, 1975. Nearby was a large army camp on both sides of the track and, while Rear and Williams in *The Cambrian Coast Railway* (ISBN 1-870119-03-7) suggest that it had its own rail network and platforms, I have been unable to corroborate their account. There was, however, to the south, a rail-served quarry, first with narrow gauge track and then converted to standard gauge.

Simplified Setrack

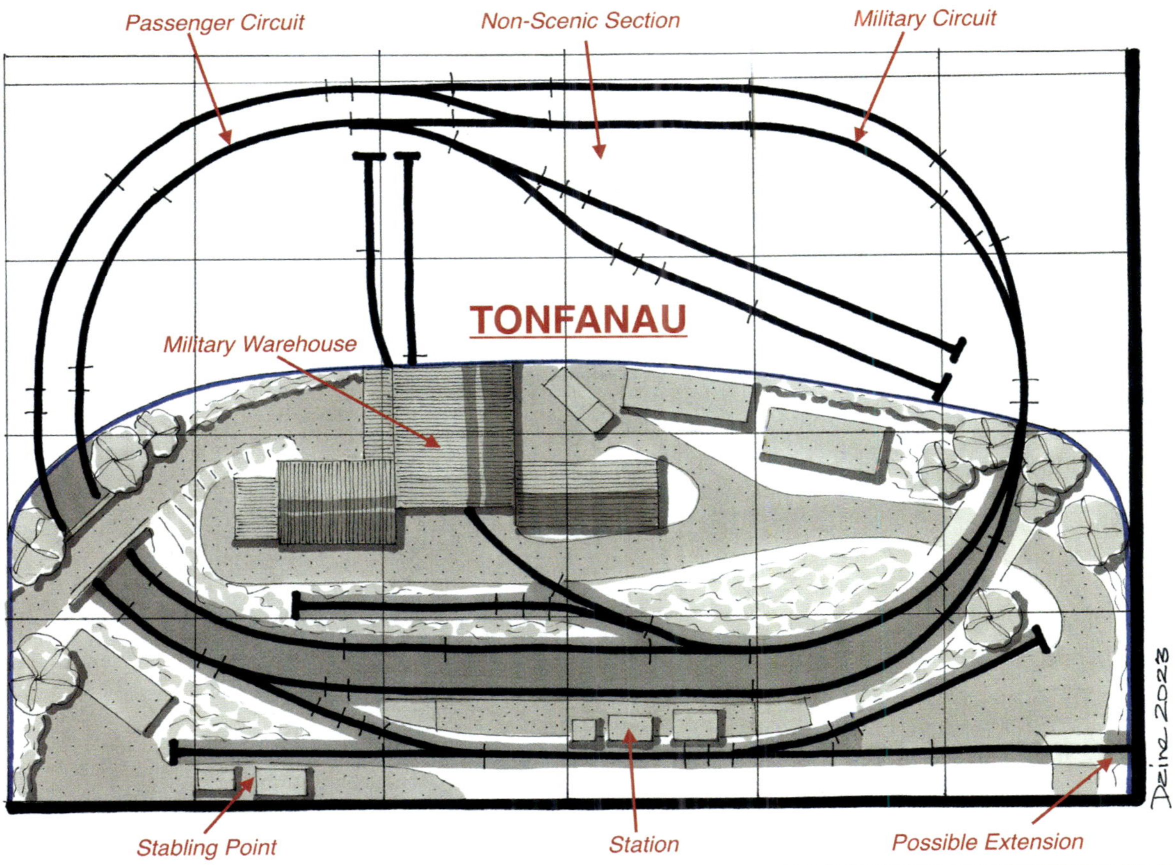

ABOVE: Never let the lack of prototype information stop you from being fictitiously creative when a good idea comes along. I refer to the military camp at Ton Fanau, which has so much potential. While I have undertaken this on the accompanying 6ft by 4ft 2in OO gauge layout, the application would work equally well for a more advanced design. I particularly like the two ovals sharing a single loop, with the outer oval for DMU passenger use and the inner for military purposes. I suggest Class 24/25-hauled in/outbound freight trains and at least one internal shunter, especially for shunting wagons into the large central warehouse and non-scenic sidings beyond, which is ideal for removing wagon loads. The front yard, with its own separate military loco, features a stabling point, although it could be a loco shed, and two sidings to the right with a hint of possible future expansion.

ABOVE AND LEFT: **Tywyn station** has a brick-built building with twin platforms and a standard GWR type 25 timber-built signal box. The latter had a gable-ended roof and 38 levers, it closed in 1988. It replaced a Cambrian version on the same site. There was also a pre-cast concrete footbridge, cattle pens, a nearby gasworks siding, coal yard in use to 1983, and an austere brick bridge dividing the station and wharf, with slate a major commodity from the Talyllyn Railway.

ABOVE LEFT AND ABOVE RIGHT: **Aberdovey station** had a passing loop and low-height platforms with a brick and stone trimmed building. The ornate cast canopy is now situated at the Bala Lake Railway at Llanuwchllyn. There was a 20 lever signal box with a corrugated roof, which closed on April 28, 1968. This was situated on the downside platform and also controlled a short branch down to the nearby harbour, which was in use to 1964. The harbour was established in the 1860s, mainly for shipping out slate and was extended by the Cambrian Railway in 1882. It was comprised of warehouses, facilities for livestock, and customs. Copper was exported and grain, timber, general goods, and cement, from the Netherlands, imported. The dock line branched off the main line east of the station, and then down a steeply graded and slightly curving route.

Simplified Setrack

The accompanying layout plan for Aberdovey Harbour mainly makes use of Setrack components, although there is a 6ft long section of flexible track employed as a static main line to the rear. At entry-level, I suggest the wagon turntables are merely cosmetic. More advanced modellers may wish to make them operational and indeed, while the trackplan is a basic one, it would easily work as a finer scale model, albeit somewhat enlarged to the proportions of the real place. The main difficulty is in view blocking the left hand end, where the branch raises up to the main line. For this arrangement. I have used a tall fictitious building to block both the exit to a fiddle yard from view and the main line overbridge behind.

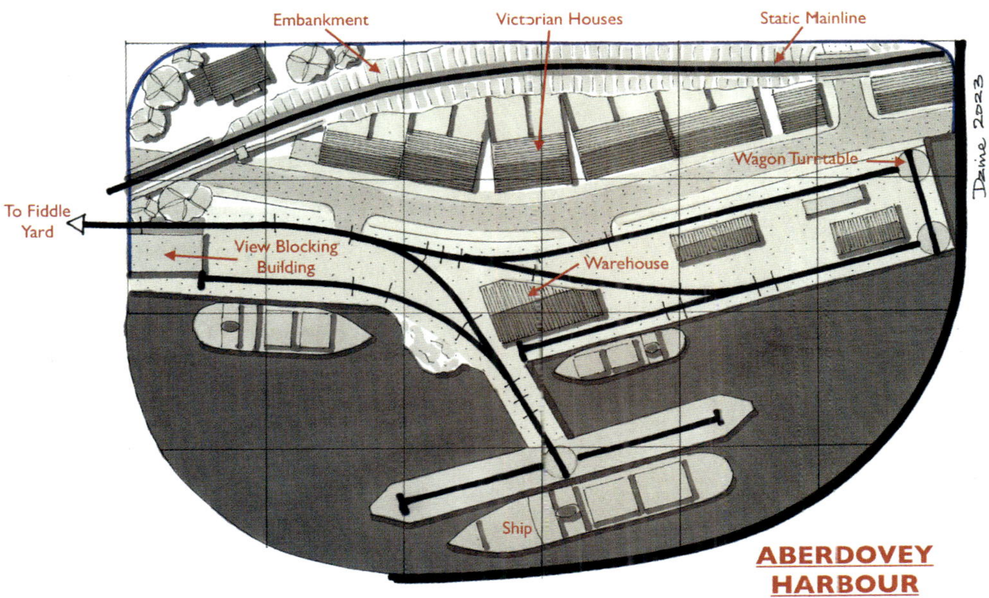

LEFT AND BELOW: **Penhelig Halt** opened on May 8, 1933, and is situated between two tunnels. The 200ft long platform is only part wooden with a GWR Pagoda-style waiting shelter and an additional lean-to, acting as an office, staffed for some of its life. A platelayer's trolley was stabled here on the short track at 90 degrees on March 23, 1976. If you are looking for a minimum space layout with an off the scale scenic arrangement and single track only, then Penhelig is the perfect place. I would either have my baseboard edge immediately in front of the track so as not to be view blocked by the long row of houses or, alternatively, reduce the houses in number so as to create a gap, or gaps, which expose the entire station scene.

LEFT: **Abertafol Halt** dates from March 18, 1935, and was renamed Abertafol on May 6, 1968. Though similar in fixtures and fittings to Gogarth, the timber hut had a pent roof and was set on a 75ft long, all-wooden platform. It was taken out of use on May 14, 1984. Note the rocky outcrop beyond the platform, as seen on March 23, 1976, which is useful as a view blocking device and a pleasant change from the overused bridge/tunnel seen on many layouts.

Gogarth Halt was built by the GWR and opened on July 9, 1923, to serve nearby campsites. It featured a typical GWR elliptical-roofed corrugated hut, set on a 99ft long all-wooden platform and a solitary nameboard and lamp on a post. A vulnerable and little-used location, mostly by school children, and surrounded by marshland, services ceased on May 14, 1984, with closure that September. A test section of model platform from recycled matchsticks and coffee stirrers was built in my *Modelling British Railways - Detailing* bookazine, available from Key Publishing.

Aberystwyth to Dovey Junction

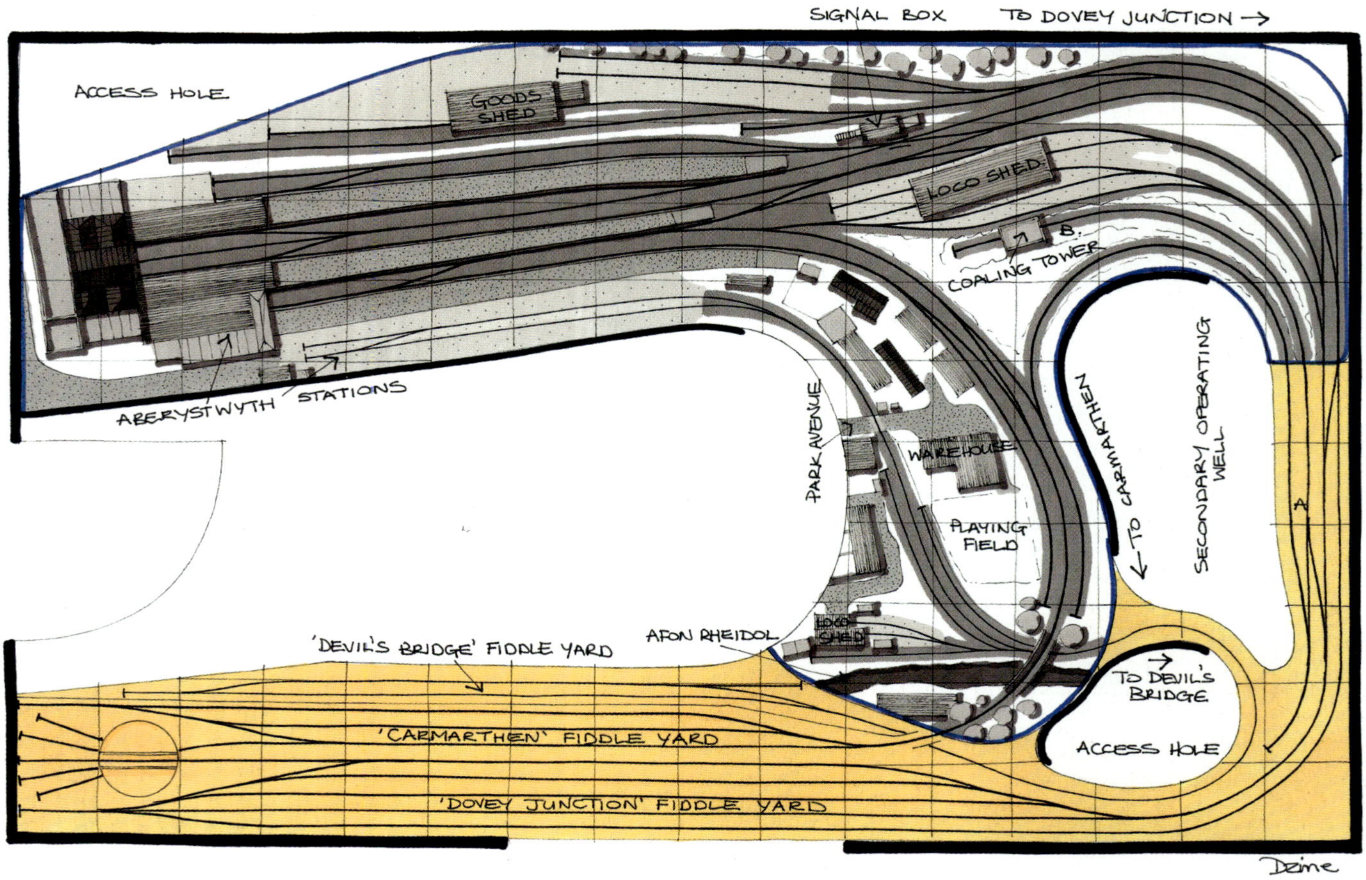

ABOVE: **Substantial prototypes are always going to demand a large space and this for Aberystwyth standard and narrow gauge railways is no exception at 16ft by 10ft. The accompanying example is for OO gauge with the neighbouring Vale of Rheidol Railway in OO9 and shows the location at its most intensive period when the Carmarthen line was still operational.**

History and description at a glance

Most of the line is across a low-lying plain, although the railway only comes close to water at Borth and River Dovey, between Ynyslas and Dovey Junction. Most stations opened on June 23, 1864. with Borth and Dovey Junction in 1863, suggesting the line was partially opened, perhaps to coincide with developing Borth as a seaside resort. Aberystwyth was always a much grander terminus than Pwllheli and the seaside resort became the most popular location on the whole of Cardigan Bay. The station is at right angles to the coast and heads inland, at first parallel to the Vale of Rheidol Railway, before heading north to Bow Street and Llandre. It then turns back out to the coast, heading northeast alongside the River Dovey and on to Dovey Junction. The largely uninhabited area here is mainly marshland and, like some other parts of North Wales, has a desolate feel about it. Operationally, timber freight traffic out of Aberystwyth has recently returned to the line and it may well be that oil traffic follows soon. As a result, there are changes already being made to the trackplan.

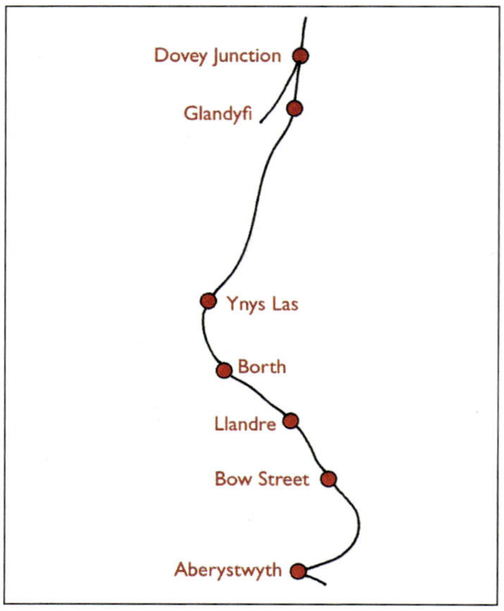

Location by location

Aberystwyth station had its terminus building added in 1924 and platforms three and four were extended to 856ft at the same time. The Carmarthen platform was also extended to 605ft, and the turntable repositioned. Services included those to Carmarthen, Shrewsbury, Birmingham, and London. There was a large loco shed, which was a sub-depot of Machynlleth and closed on April 19, 1965, the building subsequently being used by the Vale of Rheidol Railway. From 1982, the station was reduced in length from the bufferstop end, while Shell Oil's private siding was in use from August 1976 to 2011.

ABOVE AND RIGHT: **Certainly, the timetable seen here, and indeed for any time period, suggests that Dovey Junction, where two routes meet, is the best place to model if you are looking for intense activity.**

Train service

For details of additional request stops see the Train Departure poster exhibited at all stations or obtain Train Service folders from principal stations, Rail Travel Agents or Tourist information Offices.

Mondays to Saturdays / **Sundays 5 June to 4 Sept.**

		¥		A SX	SO	SX	B SO	C	SX		D SO	B SO			A SX	B SO	B SO	J	L SX	A SX	A SX	M		H		2nd Cl. only	
Pwllheli	dep.				0750	0757		0936		1040			1215			13g45			1455	1517		1600	1730		2003		
Penychain*	dep.				0758	0805		0944		1048			1223			13g53			1503	1525		1608	1738		2011		
Criccieth	dep.				0806	0813		0952		1056			1231			14g01			1511	1533		1616	1746		2019		
Porthmadog	dep.				0815	0822		1001		1105			1241			1455			1520	1542		1643	1755		2028		
Minffordd	dep.				08*19	0826				1109			1245			1459				1546		1647	1759		20*32		
Penrhyndeudraeth	dep.				0823	0830				1113			1249			1503				1550		1651	1803		2036		
Harlech	dep.				0833	0848				1123			1302			1513				1605		1704	1813		2046		
Barmouth	arr.				0852	0912				1142			1327			1532				1632		1728	1833		2106		
Barmouth	dep.			0815	0853	0917				11J43		1148	1328			1533					1734	1734	1834	2012	2109		1730
Fairbourne	dep			0824	0901	0926				11J52		1156	1337			1542					1743	1743	1843	2020	2118		1739
Llwyngwril	dep.			0832	0910	0934				12J00		1205	1345			1551					1752	1752	1851	2029	2126		
Tywyn	dep.			0848	0920	0947				12J12		1215	1358		1600	1600					1802	1802	1901	2042	2136		1756
Aberdovey	dep.			0855	0927	0954				12J18		1221	1404		1606	1606					1808	1808	1908	2049	2143		1804
Dovey Jcn.	arr.									12J33		1236									1823	1823			2158		
Borth	arr.				10a50	10b50				12f48		12f51	15b12		17b08	17b08			SX		18f38	18f38	20b23		22f13		
Aberystwyth	arr.				11a04	11b04				13f05		13f05	15b26		17b22	17b22			N	P	18f52	18f52	20b37		22f27		
Aberystwyth	dep.	0555	0750		0905D		1000		1010	12d05	1205			1400			1600	1615	1740	1750			1905			1740	
Borth	dep.	0609	0804		0919D		1016		1024	12d19	1219			1414			1616	1629	1754	1804			1920			1754	
Dovey Jcn.	dep.		0817				1030		1037	12e38	1238	1238		1427			1630	1642	1813	1817					2201		
Machynlleth	dep.	0634	0823	0917	0953	1015	1040		1048	12e45	1245	1245	1427	1434	1629	1629	1637	1649			1830	1830	1945	2110	2208	1813	1827
Caersws	dep.	0709	0858		1028		1121		1121	13e20	1320	1320		1509			1718	1724					2023			1846	1909
Newtown	dep.	0717	0907		1037		1141		1141	13e30	1330	1330		1517			1736	1736				19j21	2031			1854	1920
Welshpool	dep.	0735	0925		1055		1158		1158	13e51	1351	1351		1535			1755	1755				19j39	2051			1912	1939
Shrewsbury	arr.	0803	0959		1127		1230		1225	14e19	1419	1419		1611			1825	1825				20j07	2120			1939	2009

Mondays to Saturdays / **Sundays 5 June to 4 September**

			F		SX	SO	SX	B SO		B SO	E		A SX						2nd Cl. only	
Shrewsbury	dep.	0415					0902j	0902	1050	1226		1322		1500	1650	1834		2021	1000	1025
Welshpool	dep.	0455					0930j	0930	1120	1258		1350		1536	1718	1902		2052	1031	1053
Newtown	dep.	0520					0949j	0949	1140	1329		1409		1554	1736	1921		2111	1052	1111
Caersws	dep.	0530						0957	1148			1417		1603	1744	1929		2119	1103	1119
Machynlleth	dep.	0609	0655		0808	0849	1028G	1039	1223	1411	1435	1453	1510	1634	1815	2005	2013	2154	1139	1150
Dovey Jcn.	dep.				0818				1236						1826			2201		
Borth	dep.	0631			0830		1050G	11b04	1248	1442		1512		17m08	1838	2023		2213		1209
Aberystwyth	arr.	0652			0844		1104G	11b18	1305	1457		1526		17m22	1852	2037		2227		1222
Aberystwyth	dep.		05b55		07f50	07f50		10f00	12f05		14f00			16k15	1750H		19b05			
Borth	dep.		06b09		08f04	08f04		10f16	12f19		14f14			16k29	1804H		19b20			
Dovey Jcn.	dep.				0822	0856		1045	1237		1442			1645	1830H					
Aberdovey	dep.		0718		0839	0912		1101	1253		1457		1533	1700	1846H		2034		1202	
Tywyn	dep.		0724		0845	0926		1107	1259		1504		1605	1707	1902H		2041		1210	
Llwyngwril	dep.		0738		0859	0939		1117	1310		1514		1618	17*17	1915H		20*51			
Fairbourne	dep.		0747		0908	0948		1125	1319		1523		1627	1726	1924H		2102		1230	
Barmouth	arr.		0755		0916	0956		1133	1327		1531		1635	1734	1932H		2106		1238	
Barmouth	dep.		0817			1015h		1150	1330		1535			1740			2107			
Harlech	dep.		0846			1041h		1216	1352		1604			1814			2128			
Penrhyndeudraeth	dep.		0859			1054h		1229	1401	SX	1618			1827			2137			
Minffordd	dep.		09*02	C		1058h		12*33	1405	L	1622			1831			21*41			
Porthmadog	dep.		0906	1006		1106h		1241	1413	1525	1626			1835			2145			
Criccieth	dep.		0915	1015		1117h		1250	1424	15*34	1635			1846			2154			
Penychain*	dep.		0922	1022		1124h		1257	1431	1541	1642			1853			2201			
Pwllheli	arr.		0930	1030		1132h		1305	1442	1549	1650			1901			2209			

Notes

A – Not during School holidays.
B – 4 June to 24 September.
C – Wednesdays 8 June to 21 September.
D – Until 28 May and from 1 October.
E – Not Saturdays until 28 May and from 1 Oct.
* – Stops on request. Passengers wishing to alight must inform the Guard and those wishing to join must give a hand signal to the Driver.
F – 12 mins. earlier from Barmouth and throughout on Sats.
G – Also Saturdays until 28 May and from 1 Oct.
H – 3 June to 24 September.
J – Not Saturdays 4 June to 24 September.
L – 18 July to 5 September.
M – Mondays to Fridays during School holidays, until 15 July and from 6 September; also 18 July to 5 September; also Saturdays 4 June to 24 September.
N – Until 2 June and from 26 September.
P – 3 June to 24 September.
a – Change at Machynlleth. On Sat. 4 June to 24 Sept. arr. Borth 1104, Aberystwyth 1118.
b – Change at Machynlleth.
d – Not Sats. 7 to 28 May and from 1 Oct. Change at Dovey Jcn.
e – Mondays to Fridays.
f – Change at Dovey Jcn.
g – Change at Porthmadog.
h – Runs Mondays to Fridays.
i – Mons. to Fridays 18 July to 5 Sept. and Saturdays 4 June to 24 September.
k – Change at Dovey Jcn. on Sats. 4 June to 24 Sept. dep. Aberystwyth 1600 Borth 1616.
m – Not Sats. 7 to 28 May and from 1 Oct. Mons. to Fridays change at Machynlleth.
¥ – Does not run Bank Holidays.

Children 3 and under 14 years half fare unless otherwise stated (under 3 free). The fares quoted are second class unless first class fares are indicated.

All facilities shown in this folder are subject to alteration or cancellation. The prices shown are those in force at the time of printing, and are liable to alteration, current prices can be obtained from British Rail Stations Travel Offices and appointed Travel Agents.

Published by British Rail
Printed by Clement & Foster Ltd.
N1246

ABOVE: **An inbound Carmarthen three-coach train, hauled by 80101, on August 24, 1964. Note there is a second loco of the same class, already attached for the outward journey.** Richard Inwood/Paul A Lunn Collection

ABOVE: **The original station with cast canopy before shortening. Note the three track arrangement. A Class 101 DMU with a Mk.1 CCT as tail traffic awaits departure to Machynlleth on September 15, 1976.**

LEFT: **Staff wait with a substantial amount of bagged mail for the next inbound train on the same date. The intricate security gates make this a particularly attractive scene, although they would be fiddly to model.**

ABOVE: The track layout was controlled by a Dutton & Co. 100-lever brick and timber signal box, which closed on April 25, 1982.

ABOVE: BR large logo blue-liveried 37430 *Cwmbran* hauled an InterCity five-coach special on August 18, 1986. Note the rationalised platform trackwork.

ABOVE: Network Rail's 31602 at Aberystwyth with a test train. Suitably-liveried locos are available from Hornby, Graham Farish and, shortly, Accurascale. The coach immediately behind the loco is QXA 999508, a 57ft long former inspection saloon modified as a track recording coach in the mid-1980s. This was withdrawn from traffic in 2013.

Bow Street station closed on June 14, 1965, while the signal box and loop were taken out of use on March 3, 1968. Some sidings were in use up to September 1964. There was a GWR camping coach provided from 1934 to 1939 and from BR's Western Region, a coach from 1952 to 1957, with two present in 1958/59. The station was re-opened from February 14, 2021, south of the original site.

RIGHT: **Llandre station** closed on June 14, 1965, having originally been named Llanfihangel until 1916. The stone station building still remains as a private dwelling and, although the loop was taken out of use and signal box closed on August 20, 1966, it was still in place at the time of my photo on September 15, 1976.

RIGHT: **Borth station** opened on July 1, 1863. It had two platforms, the main one built from concrete blocks and a second of wooden trestle construction. Part of the original brick-built station building is used for railway purposes with the rest given over to commercial use. A Dutton & Co. signal box along with the loop were taken out of use from November 4, 1973. There was also a goods yard to the north. The GWR provided a camping coach between 1934-39 and the Western Region from 1952 to 1968, with two in place from 1969 to 1971.

ABOVE: **Ynyslas station** was a rendered building with slate roof and now demolished; note the low height platform. The other platform, still in use at the time of this photo, is a full height timber-stockade back-filled and topped off with chippings. Cattle pens were added in January 1872, while goods and parcel services ceased in 1938 and the signal box and loop were taken out of use from September 15, 1963.

ABOVE: **Glandyfi** (Glandovey). By the time of my only visit here, the house was in a reasonable state but the same could not be said for the station building. In this contrasting condition, it would make for an unusual model. The signal box was taken out of use from August 7, 1966, with all other tracks, apart from the main line, following on September 28, 1964.

Dovey Junction opened in 1863 as Glandovey Junction, being re-named in 1904. Passenger access is via a footpath only alongside the Aberystwyth line, from the A487 near Derwenlas. The original Cambrian Railway buildings were removed in 1958/59. The pre-fabricated concrete station building dates from that time and was replaced in the 1970s by flat-roof structures. These gave way to a platform 'bus shelter' in the 1990s with the platforms raised in height during 2008.

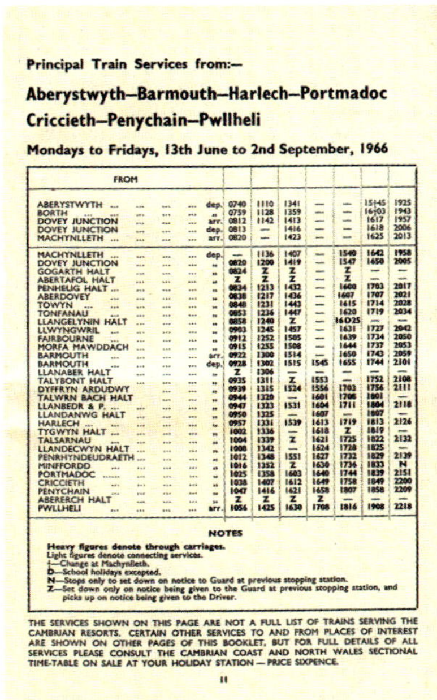

Principal Train Services from:–

Aberystwyth–Barmouth–Harlech–Portmadoc Criccieth–Penychain–Pwllheli

Mondays to Fridays, 13th June to 2nd September, 1966

FROM								
ABERYSTWYTH	dep.	0740	1110	1341	—	—	15‡45	1925
BORTH	"	0759	1128	1359	—	—	16‡03	1943
DOVEY JUNCTION	arr.	0812	1142	1413	—	—	1617	1957
DOVEY JUNCTION	dep.	0813	—	1416	—	—	1618	2006
MACHYNLLETH	arr.	0820	—	1423	—	—	1625	2013
MACHYNLLETH	dep.	—	1136	1407	—	1540	1642	1958
DOVEY JUNCTION	"	0820	1200	1419	—	1547	1650	2005
GOGARTH HALT	"	0824	Z	Z	—	Z	—	—
ABERTAFOL HALT	"	Z	Z	Z	—	Z	—	—
PENHELIG HALT	"	0834	1213	1432	—	1600	1703	2017
ABERDOVEY	"	0838	1217	1436	—	1607	1707	2021
TOWYN	"	0848	1231	1443	—	1615	1714	2028
TONFANAU	"	0853	1236	1447	—	1620	1719	2034
LLANGELYNIN HALT	"	0858	1240	Z	—	16D25	—	—
LLWYNGWRIL	"	0903	1245	1457	—	1631	1727	2042
FAIRBOURNE	"	0912	1252	1505	—	1639	1734	2050
MORFA MAWDDACH	"	0915	1255	1508	—	1644	1737	2053
BARMOUTH	arr.	0922	1300	1514	—	1650	1743	2059
BARMOUTH	dep.	0928	1302	1515	1545	1655	1744	2101
LLANABER HALT	"	Z	1306	—	—	—	—	—
TALYBONT HALT	"	0935	1311	Z	1553	—	1752	2108
DYFFRYN ARDUDWY	"	0939	1315	1524	1556	1702	1756	2111
TALWRN BACH HALT	"	0944	1320	—	1601	1708	1801	—
LLANBEDR & P.	"	0947	1323	1531	1604	1711	1804	2118
LLANDANWG HALT	"	0950	1325	—	1607	—	1807	—
HARLECH	"	0957	1331	1539	1613	1719	1813	2126
TYGWYN HALT	"	1002	1336	—	1618	Z	1819	—
TALSARNAU	"	1004	1339	Z	1621	1725	1822	2132
LLANDECWYN HALT	"	1008	1342	—	1624	1728	1825	—
PENRHYNDEUDRAETH	"	1012	1348	1551	1627	1732	1829	2139
MINFFORDD	"	1016	1352	Z	1630	1736	1833	N
PORTMADOC	"	1025	1358	1603	1640	1744	1839	2151
CRICCIETH	"	1038	1407	1612	1649	1758	1849	2200
PENYCHAIN	"	1047	1416	1621	1658	1807	1858	2209
ABERERCH HALT	"	Z	Z	Z	Z	—	—	—
PWLLHELI	arr.	1056	1425	1630	1708	1816	1908	2218

NOTES

Heavy figures denote through carriages.
Light figures denote connecting services.
‡—Change at Machynlleth.
D—School holidays excepted.
N—Stops only to set down on notice to Guard at previous stopping station.
Z—Set down only on notice being given to the Guard at previous stopping station, and picks up on notice being given to the Driver.

THE SERVICES SHOWN ON THIS PAGE ARE NOT A FULL LIST OF TRAINS SERVING THE CAMBRIAN RESORTS. CERTAIN OTHER SERVICES TO AND FROM PLACES OF INTEREST ARE SHOWN ON OTHER PAGES OF THIS BOOKLET, BUT FOR FULL DETAILS OF ALL SERVICES PLEASE CONSULT THE CAMBRIAN COAST AND NORTH WALES SECTIONAL TIME-TABLE ON SALE AT YOUR HOLIDAY STATION — PRICE SIXPENCE.

11

ABOVE LEFT AND ABOVE RIGHT: 80136 with a three-coach train stands at the platform for Aberystwyth on August 26, 1964. The accompanying timetable gives an idea of the principal services around this period. Richard Inwood/Paul A Lunn Collection

ABOVE: These three photos, all with the 11.36 Machynlleth to Pwllheli DMU, were taken on March 23, 1976, and give a clear indication of the stretch of line from the timber trestle bridge over the River Dovey to the western end of the station.

ABOVE LEFT AND ABOVE RIGHT: There were sidings at the eastern end of Dovey Junction and a wonderful group of semaphore signals. I include a close up to aid modelmaking.

ABOVE: The station featured a BR type 37, 65-lever GWR pattern frame, ply, and timber platform-mounted signal box, this being pre-fabricated with 6ft panels and vertical planking. The original timber trackside box had a Dutton & Co. 52-lever frame.

LEFT: Set 158828 in the Aberystwyth platform as my train passes by. There is much more ground cover here now in 2023 than in the 1970s.

More modelling inspiration

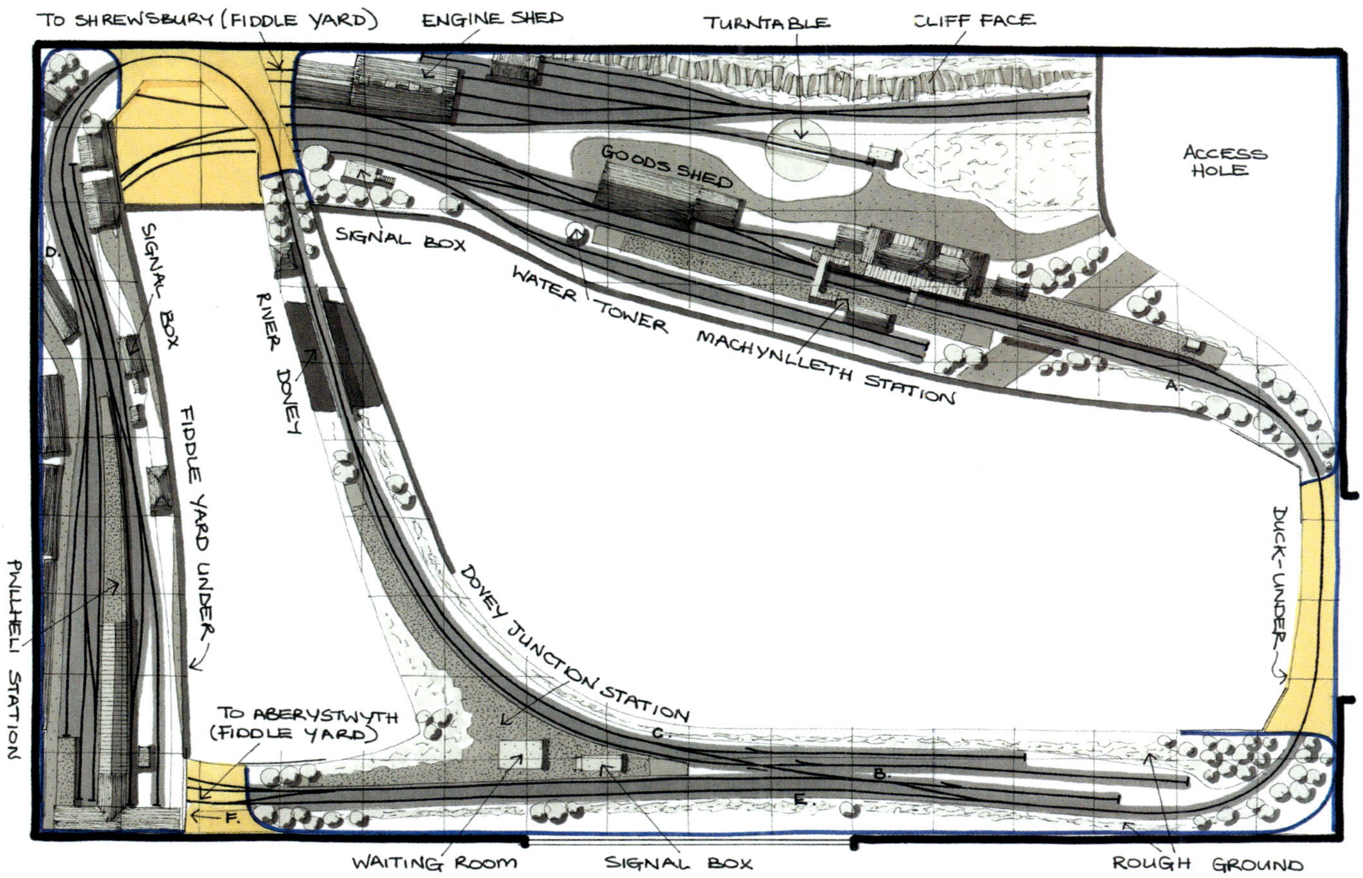

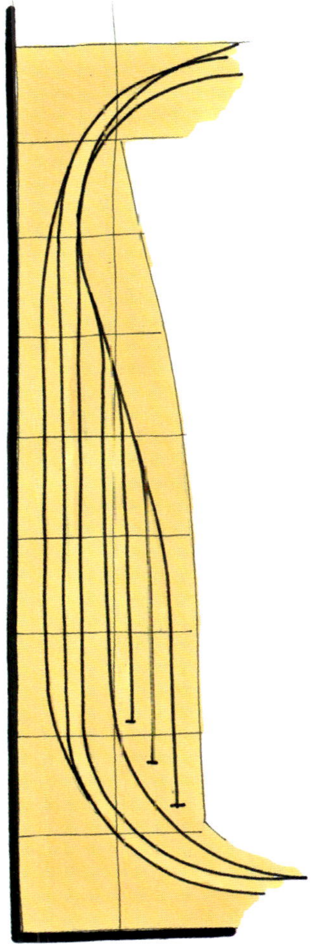

ABOVE AND RIGHT: **A second 16ft by 10ft OO gauge layout, again large in size but comprising three stations with a low-level fiddle yard. As such, there are gradients and, depending on train length, these might need help from DCC Concepts' Power Base system. These are steep in order to provide sufficient clearance between Pwllheli station and the fiddle yard, with gradients up from A to B, C to D and down E to F, with F being near the right hand point, bottom left, on the fiddle yard detail plan. In the main, I have stayed faithful to the real stations, compromising on second radius curves at both ends of Machynlleth station, with one each at Dovey and Pwllheli. This is worth it for operational value though, while many of the tight curves are either non-scenic or masked by tree grouping. If you are looking for something smaller, then modern-day Aberystwyth, a radically compressed Dovey Junction, or any other station, most likely Borth with its long operational freight time span to 1973, would more than suffice in oval format, or as an 'L' shaped Aberystwyth to fiddle yard only.**

Llandudno Junction to Blaenau Ffestiniog

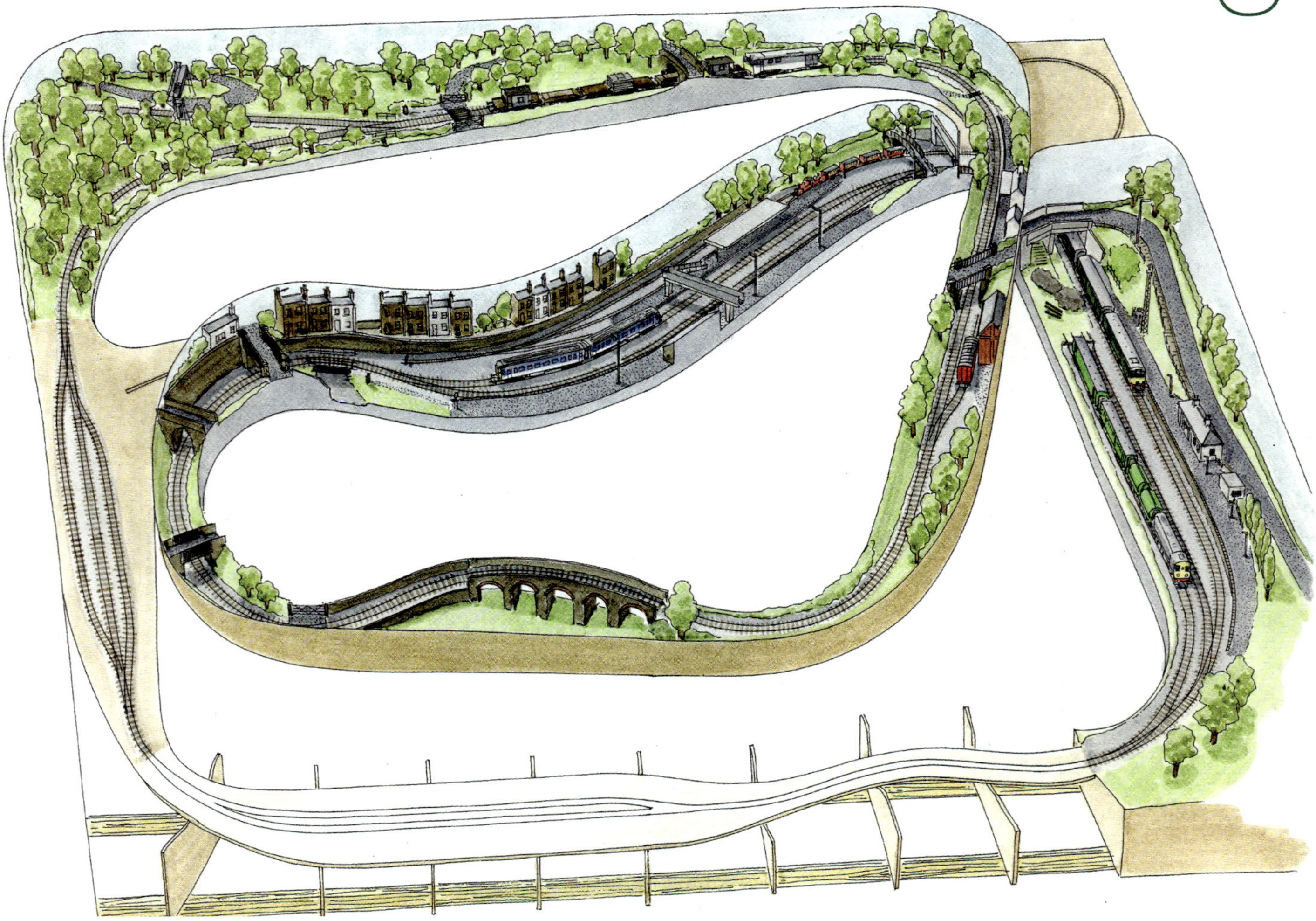

LEFT AND ABOVE: **This OO gauge 3D illustration shows a model interpretation running from Llanwrst (open top baseboard at bottom left) to Blaenau Ffestiniog (LNWR, right) and Blaenau Ffestiniog Interchange with a section of the narrow gauge line (upper central section). Also included are Manod Viaduct (lower central section), Maentwrog Road (with red brick goods shed), the truncated Trawsfynydd Power Station line with nuclear flask gantry crane along the top, and a modest three-loop fiddle yard (left). It occupies a space of 15ft by 12ft with one level looping over the other at the top right hand corner. While the arrangement is for the 1990s, you could choose a different period, such as the BR mid-late 1950s, similar to the accompanying pamphlet.**

History and description at a glance

The line traverses the Conwy and Lledr valleys and is 27.25 miles long. There are stunning scenic views of Foel Fras, part of Carnedd Llewellyn, and only slightly smaller than Snowdon. The section from Llandudno Junction to Llanwrst opened on June 1, 1863, and was taken over by the LNWR in the same year. An extension to Betws-y-Coed took place from April 6, 1868, with the station being a terminus to 1876. The final section to Blaenau Ffestiniog was added on April 1, 1881.

Slate has been a key part of the line's industry and indeed Blaenau Ffestiniog is renowned for the slate spoil heaps. Slate reached its peak in the 1890s when Oakeley Mine was reported to be the largest in the world and was well known for its interchange, near to the southern portal of Blaenau Ffestiniog Tunnel. Demand decreased thereafter due to production costs and roof tile manufacturing, with the industry having contracted by half by 1914. Slate extraction has returned to Oakeley

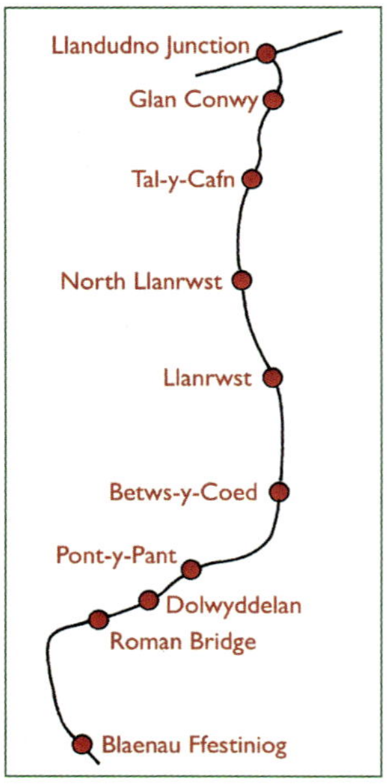

and Llechwedd Quarry and is operated by McAlpine. DMUs were first allocated to the line from March 5, 1956, while general freight ended from May 4, 1964, but wagonload freight continued to 1982. Specials, steam-hauled charter trains, logging, nuclear waste, gunpowder, and aluminium have all featured on the line over the decades. From June 14, 1994, for about a year, two Queen Mary brake vans were kept at Llandudno Junction for use on trains re-ballasting the branch.

Location by location

Llandudno Junction is where the branch diverges from the Chester end of the station and past these sidings, then given over to engineers' use. The area was subsequently redeveloped to accommodate the A55. Beyond, the line traverses marshland until it joins the Conwy river bank.

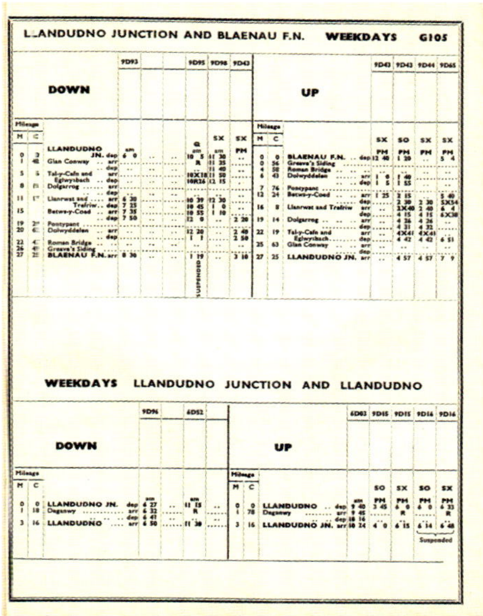

LLANDUDNO JUNCTION AND BLAENAU F.N. **WEEKDAYS** G105

DOWN

M	C			9D93			9D95	9D98	9D43
							Q	SX	SX
				am			am	am	PM
0	3	LLANDUDNO JN.	dep	6 0	..	..	10 5	11 30	..
1	48	Glan Conway	arr				R	11 35	
			dep	..	..	..	..	11 40	..
5	[illegible]	Tal-y-Cafn and	arr				10X18	11 50	
		Eglwysbach	dep	..	..	..	10R26	12 15	.
8	[illegible]	Dolgarrog	arr						
			dep	..	..	..	..	..	..
11	[illegible]	Llanrwst and	arr	6 30			10 39	12 30	
		Trefriw	dep	7 25	..	..	10 45	1 0	..
15		Betws-y-Coed	arr	7 35			10 55	1 10	
			dep	7 50	..	..	12 0	..	2 20
19	[illegible]	Pontypant							
20	[illegible]	Dolwyddelan	arr	..	..	..	12 20	..	2 40
			dep				1 1		2 50
22	[illegible]	Roman Bridge		..	..	..	..	..	..
26	[illegible]	Greave's Siding							
27	[illegible]	BLAENAU F.N.	arr	8 30	..	..	1 19	..	3 10
							SUSPENDED		

UP

M	C			9D43	9D43	9D44	9D65
				SX	SO	SX	SX
				PM	PM	PM	PM
0	0	BLAENAU F.N.	dep	12 40	1 20	..	5 4
0	56	Greave's Siding					
4	58	Roman Bridge		..	..	..	..
6	43	Dolwyddelan	arr	1 0	1 40		
			dep	1 5	1 55	..	..
7	76	Pontypant					
12	24	Betws-y-Coed	arr	1 25	2 15	..	5 40
			dep		2 30	2 30	5X54
16	8	Llanrwst and Trefriw	arr	..	3X40	2 40	6 4
			dep		4 15	4 15	6X30
19	14	Dolgarrog	arr	..	4 26	4 26	..
			dep		4 31	4 32	
22	19	Tal-y-Cafn and	arr	..	4X41	4X41	..
		Eglwysbach	dep		4 42	4 42	6 51
25	63	Glan Conway	arr	..	..	..	..
			dep				
27	25	LLANDUDNO JN.	arr	..	4 57	4 57	7 9

WEEKDAYS LLANDUDNO JUNCTION AND LLANDUDNO

DOWN

M	C			9D96		6D52	
				am		am	
0	0	LLANDUDNO JN.	dep	6 27	..	11 15	..
1	18	Deganwy	arr	6 32		R	
			dep	6 41	..	..	..
3	16	LLANDUDNO	arr	6 50		11 30	

UP

M	C			6D83	9D15	9D15	9D16	9D16
					SO	SX	SO	SX
				am	PM	PM	PM	PM
0	0	LLANDUDNO	dep	9 40	3 45	6 0	6 0	6 33
1	78	Deganwy	arr	9 45		R		R
			dep	10 16	..	..	..	..
3	16	LLANDUDNO JN.	arr	10 24	4 0	6 15	6 14	6 48
							Suspended	Suspended

LEFT: **Glan Conway station opened as Llansaintffraid on June 17, 1863, before it was re-named from the beginning of 1865. It was closed to passenger traffic from October 26, 1964, and reopened again on May 4, 1970. There was a single siding for coal and agricultural traffic and a camping coach was sited here from 1954 to 1964.**

RIGHT: Taly y Cafn and Eglwsbach station is seen on May 6, 1974, after renaming to the more manageable Tal-y-Cafn. The station building was almost identical to Glan Conway, and the manually-operated level crossing gates were still in use. In the past, there were cattle pens, sheds, and a timber wharf, which is ideal for a more interesting model interpretation.

Dolgarrog Halt was built by the LNWR and opened on January 1, 1917. It closed briefly in October 1964 but re-opened the following June. In the past, it had a waiting room, small office, and platelayer's hut on the opposite side of the track at the northern end, but now it is a modern, long-ramped uncluttered platform.

About a mile away, Aluminium Corporation Ltd opened a works in 1908 to convert bauxite into aluminium. Hydro-electric power from nearby reservoirs was used to operate the rolling mills, pressing aluminium sheet to a variety of thicknesses. While there had been a previous narrow gauge system, a standard gauge line was built from Dolgarrog Halt in 1916. It commenced at some interchange sidings before turning approximately 180 degrees and crossed over a shared road/river steel bridge, and then headed north to the works.

Here there were numerous buildings and a loco shed. The whole site was taken over by the Ministry of Defence during the Second World War when there was great demand for aluminium for the construction of aircraft bodies. There was considerable expansion during this time and rail traffic increased dramatically. For military modellers, anti-aircraft guns were brought on-site, pillboxes were erected and there was much camouflaging undertaken on the works and nearby village. The British Aluminium Company took over in 1949 but traffic ceased during the early 1960s with the track lifted during 1963. The works closed during 2007 and was subsequently demolished.

The accompanying OO gauge 10ft by 7ft trackplan captures much of the original, albeit in an oval format. I have included a short section of narrow gauge line for added interest and please note the standard gauge curve next to the hand access hole is first radius. The internal railway

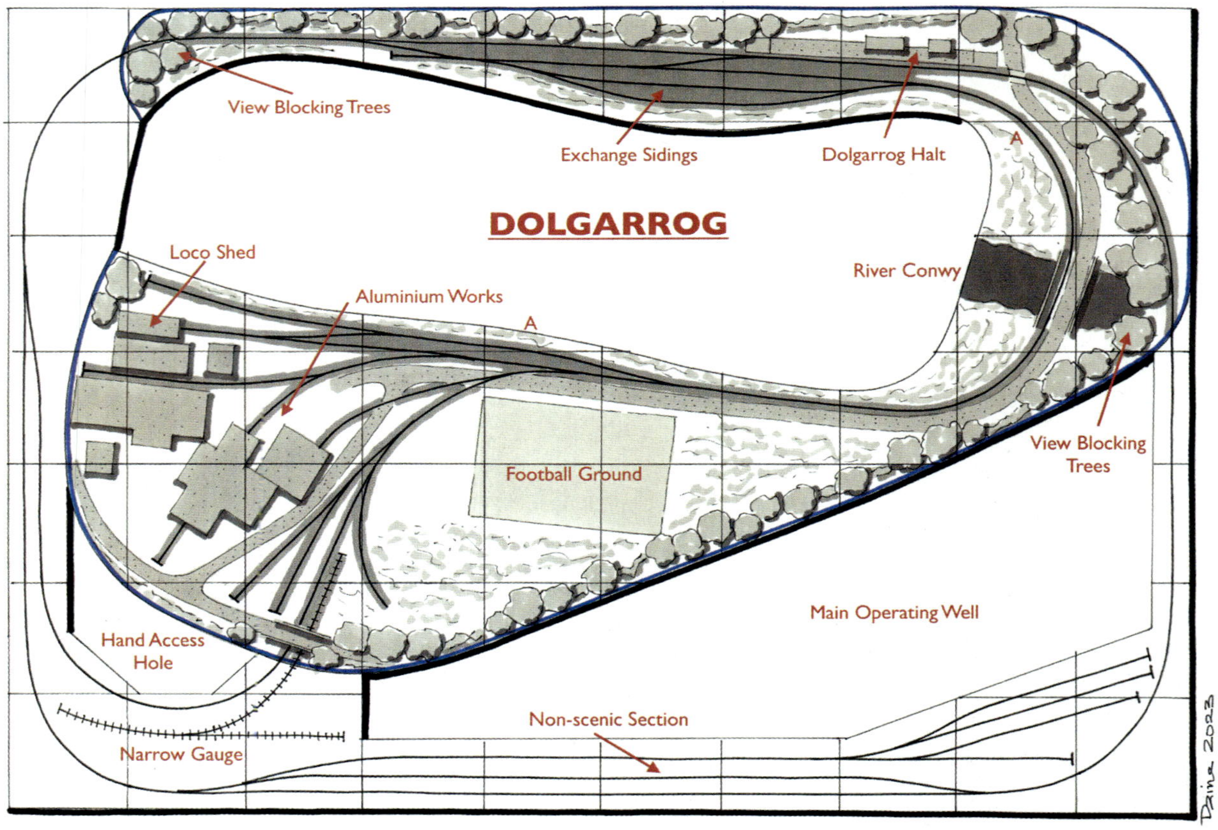

had two stations with low to the ground platforms. Despite my best efforts, I have been unable to ascertain their exact locations. I am guessing they were roughly in the positions marked A but note the one nearest Dolgarrog Halt was possibly on a curved loop, which I had insufficient space to include in my design, between the exchange sidings and the River Conwy bridge.

Locos and stock

- *Uxbridge*, a 0-6-0ST built by Hunslet Engine Co. in 1902, scrapped in 1952.
- *Dolgarrog*, a 0-6-0ST Manning Wardle built in 1901, had left by 1928.
- *Dolgarrog No. 1* from Robert Stevenson & Hawthornes Ltd, built in 1943, scrapped in 1962.

The line was worked one engine in steam, as and when required. There may have been ten wagons, possibly internal users, although again this is not clear. Passenger services operated from 1917 to 1932 and made use of two coaches: one a four-wheel ex-North London Railway design and the other one a bogie coach.

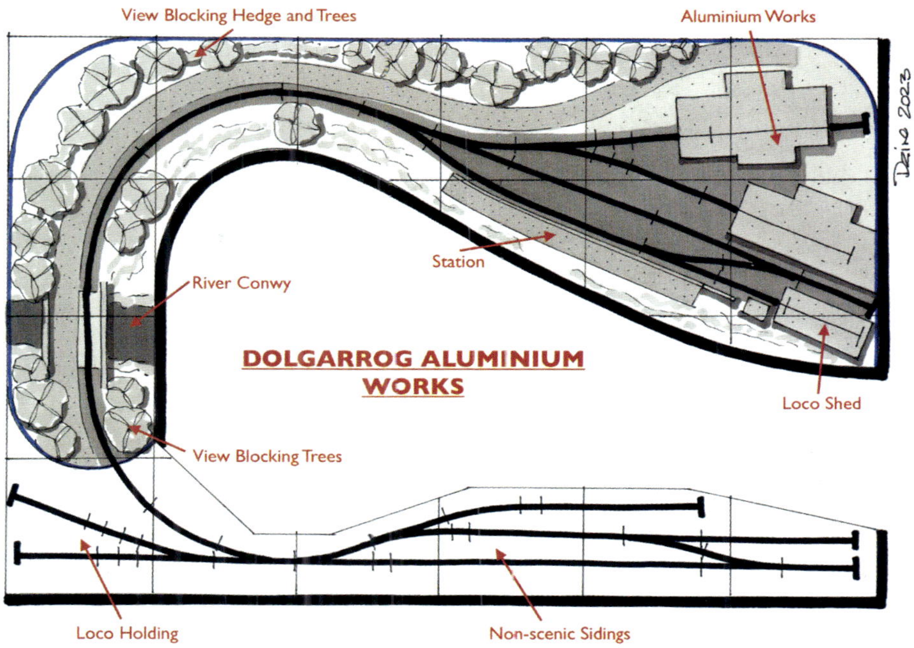

Simplified Setrack

A 'U' shaped arrangement occupying a space of 6ft by 4ft in OO. While much compressed and void of Dolgarrog Halt itself, there is opportunity for some outstanding scenic treatment in the section from the bottom left-hand corner to the works yard entrance. Please note that access to the central operating well is via a sideways shuffle through a gap; those portl er may have to duck under!

Llanwrst station opened from June 17, 1863, but was re-sited five years later. It was re-named Llanwrst and Trefriw in April 1884 before becoming Llanrwst on May 6, 1974. Two further name changes have since occurred, firstly to **Llanrwst North** from July 29, 1989, and currently **North Llanrwst** from December 2004. It had a goods yard with five sidings, a brick and timber signal box, and low-height platforms with steps. The passing loop is now the only one on the line and there is a short tunnel to the south of the station.

RIGHT: **Llanwrst station** opened in 1989, being sited half a mile away from North Llanwrst. It is a basic modern, step-free, single concrete platform with a stone bridge immediately to the north.

Back in time

Betws-y-Coed station opened in 1868 with full length up and down platforms and was the main station on the line with a large goods yard, primarily for slate traffic. Some trains used to terminate here and there was a camping coach from 1955 to 1959, this being replaced by a Pullman coach from 1960 to 1970. The passing loop was removed during the 1960s and the footbridge, originally between both platforms, now gives access to Conwy Valley Railway Museum and miniature railway, which was established in the early 1970s. It is an important tourist location with spectacular scenery and waterfalls, including swallow falls nearby. The section of line after Betws-y-Coed is on a gradient rising 700ft in ten miles, with sections at 1:60, 1:50 and 1:47, alongside Gwydyr Forest, before crossing Pont Gethin Viaduct and on to Pont-y-Pant Lower Tunnel.

Pont Gethin Viaduct spans the Ledr Valley. It was built between 1877-79 in a Scots Baronial style with multiple castel ated safety refuges. Mainly constructed from stone and featuring one large and seven smaller arches, it is 1,070ft long, which is approximately 4.28 metres in OO gauge. The building contractor was Owain Gethin Jones, hence the name.

Pont y Pant station opened on July 22, 1879. There was a loop until 1951 and a siding with a headshunt for loading slate from the Rhiw-Goch Quarry. There were further sidings to the north of the station and the River Lledr nearby, with outstanding views of Moel Siabod. The LMS had a caravan here between 1934-36 and two from 1937 to 1939, plus a camping coach around 1954.

Dolwddellan station opened 1879 and had an island platform, though it is now single track only. There was a goods yard, including a shed, on waste ground to the left and a water column. The now demolished substantial station building was accessed from steps and a span up to the nearby road. On the north side of the road overbridge. There is a bridge over a tributary off the Afon Lledr, seen in the accompanying photo. There was a narrow gauge incline serving Ty'n-y-Bryn Quarries, near the fourth telegraph pole, down the right hand side. The railway climbs from here at 1:62 to the summit of the line, inside a tunnel 790ft above sea level.

Roman Bridge station opened on July 22, 1879, and is the last station in the Lledr Valley before Ffestiniog Tunnel. It is a small station and had a siding, which was lifted by the mid-1960s, with an adjacent lever frame. Two LMS caravans were sited here from 1935 to 1939 and a camping coach from 1954 to 1956. The station buildings still survive in what is a remote area.

Over the years

RIGHT: **Ffestiniog Tunnel**, built between 1873 and 1879, is 2.5 miles long and cut through slate bedrock. It is the longest un-lined tunnel in the UK and prone to rock falls, although some reinforcement with stainless steel rock bolts has taken place in more recent times. The southern portal is of dressed stone and has a semi-circular arch and pediment with an engineer's plaque reading 'W. Smith 1879.'

ABOVE: The ex LNWR station at **Blaenau Ffestiniog** opened on April 1, 1881, and became **Blaenau Ffestiniog North** in 1951 and **Blaenau Ffestiniog** once again from May 6, 1968, when the former GWR station, Blaenau Ffestiniog Central, closed. The ex LNWR station itself closed from March 22, 1982, when the new interchange opened. It consisted of a single platform, an extensive goods yard and interchange with narrow gauge, mainly for slate workings and coal. There were two goods sheds (one with a narrow gauge interchange), a hand-operated turntable, and an engine and carriage shed. The original signal box was large and tall to give a clear view, although it was replaced by 1949 with a smaller version. The station building was originally timber but succumbed to a fire in 1951. A permanent replacement was provided during 1956 and there were cattle pens and stables. It was used as a passenger interchange with nearby narrow gauge lines at Ffestiniog Junction to 1939. The narrow gauge line from Oakeley Quarry to the LNWR/LMS exchange sidings continued to be used up to the mid-1960s and the area is well known for its surrounding slate tips, despite some waste material having been removed during 2002.

Link across Blaenau. To serve the nuclear power station at Trawsfynydd, a link line was built from the LNWR station using part of the narrow gauge trackbed, through the village and to the old Central station site. This connected with the northern remnants of the Blaenau to Bala line, running to a two siding terminal near Llyn Trawsfynydd, which was an artificial reservoir for the power station. The line beyond this point closed in January 1960.

Back in time

Blaenau Ffestiniog interchange station. Both British Rail and the Ffestiniog Railway agreed on the benefits of a new interchange station, near where the ex-GWR Central station had been. The arrangement pictured here dates from March 22, 1982, with the ex-LNWR station closing the same day. The black and white image dates from the previous decade. The narrow gauge line opened from May 1982.

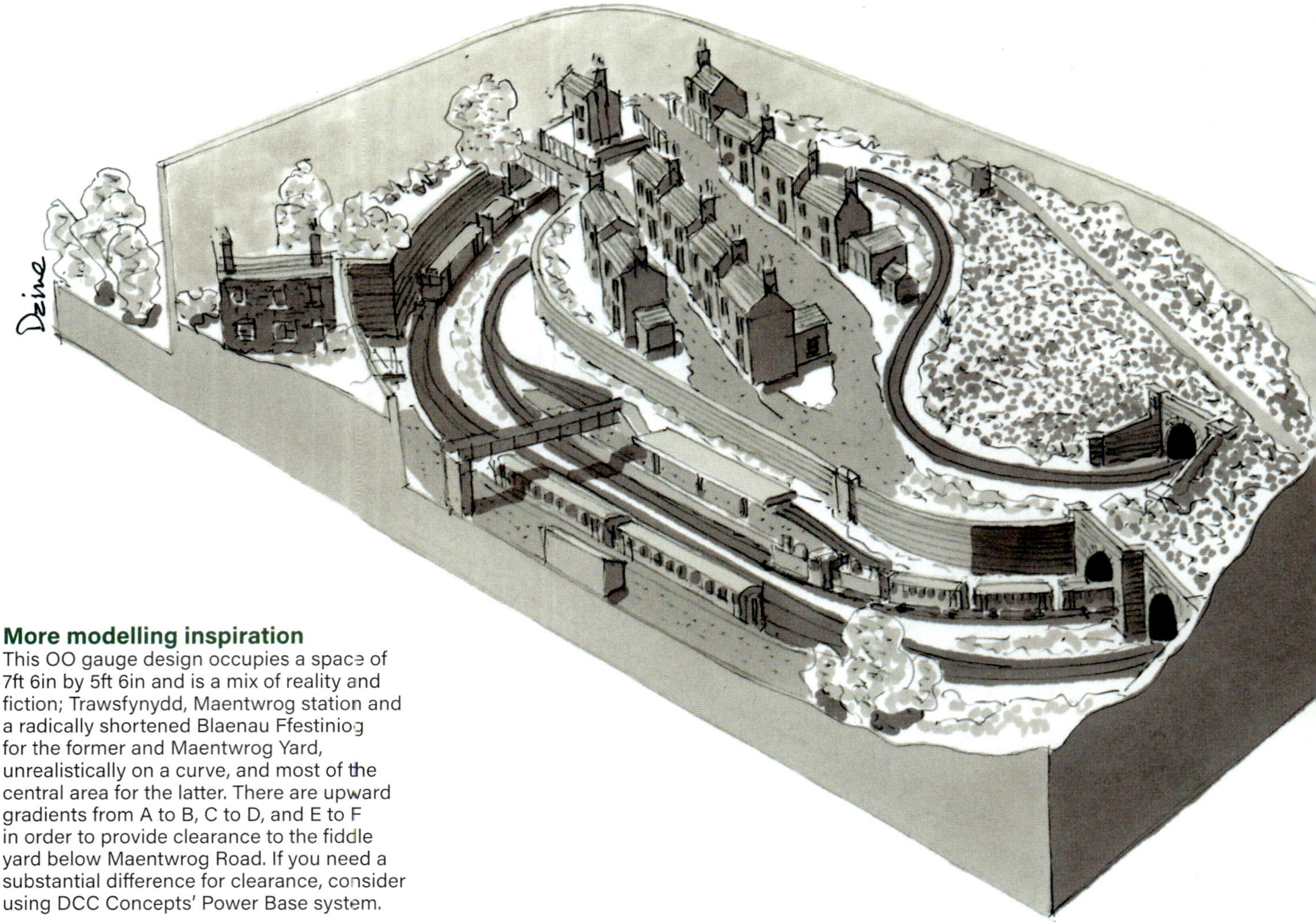

More modelling inspiration

This OO gauge design occupies a space of 7ft 6in by 5ft 6in and is a mix of reality and fiction; Trawsfynydd, Maentwrog station and a radically shortened Blaenau Ffestiniog for the former and Maentwrog Yard, unrealistically on a curve, and most of the central area for the latter. There are upward gradients from A to B, C to D, and E to F in order to provide clearance to the fiddle yard below Maentwrog Road. If you need a substantial difference for clearance, consider using DCC Concepts' Power Base system.

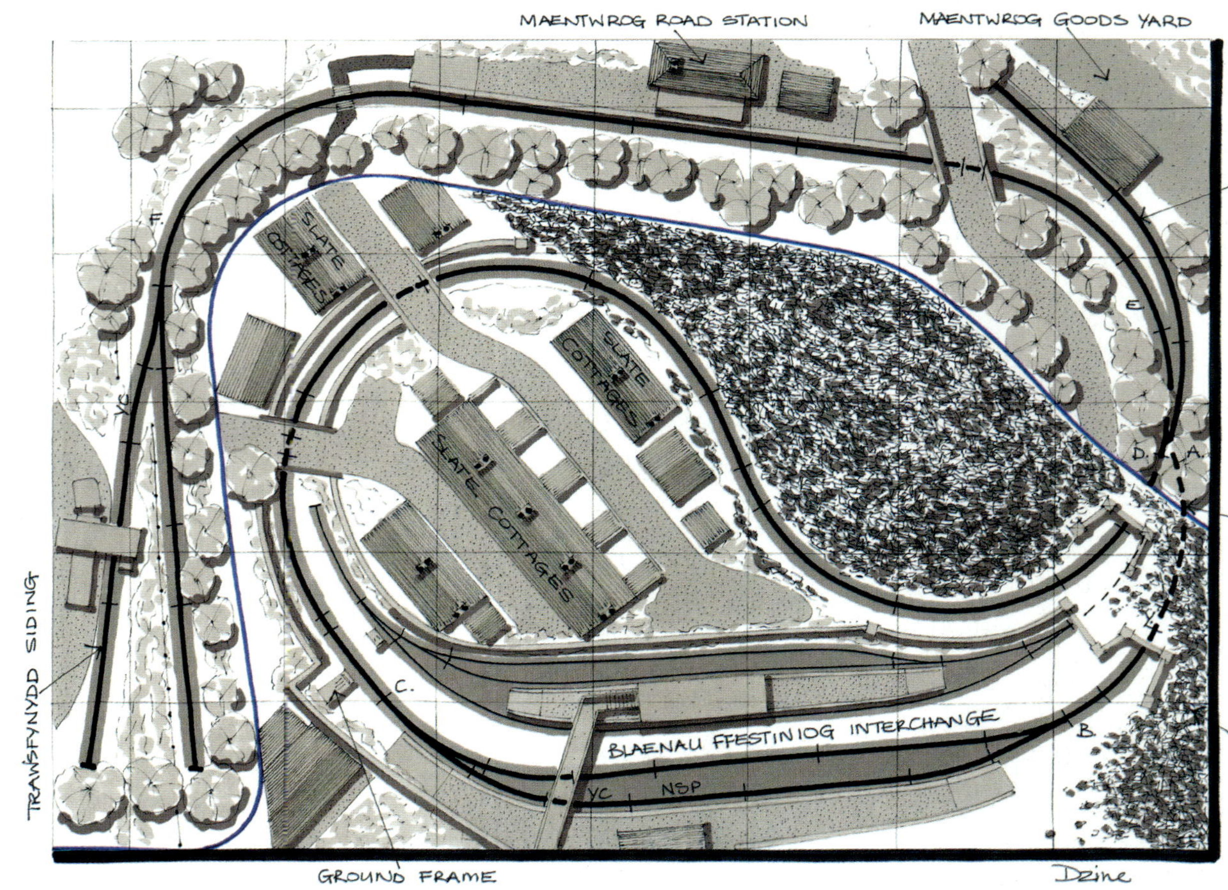

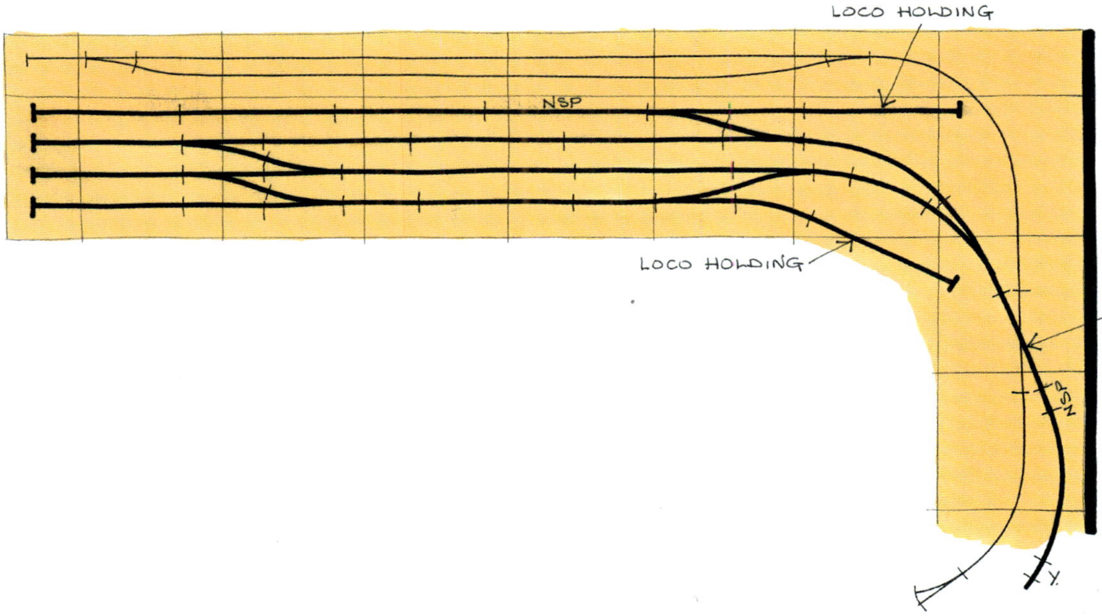

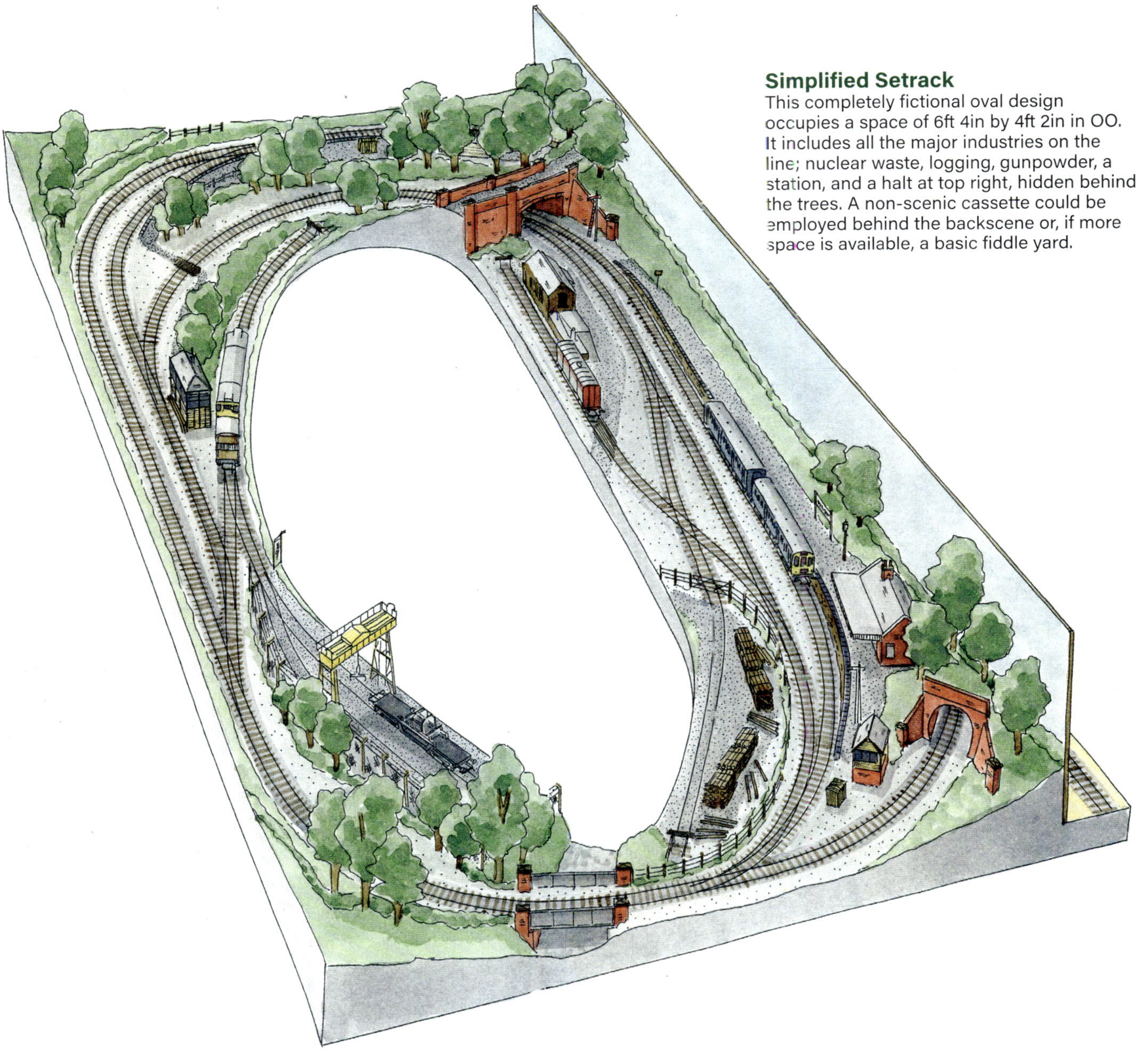

Simplified Setrack
This completely fictional oval design occupies a space of 6ft 4in by 4ft 2in in OO. It includes all the major industries on the line; nuclear waste, logging, gunpowder, a station, and a halt at top right, hidden behind the trees. A non-scenic cassette could be employed behind the backscene or, if more space is available, a basic fiddle yard.

Blaenau Ffestiniog to Bala

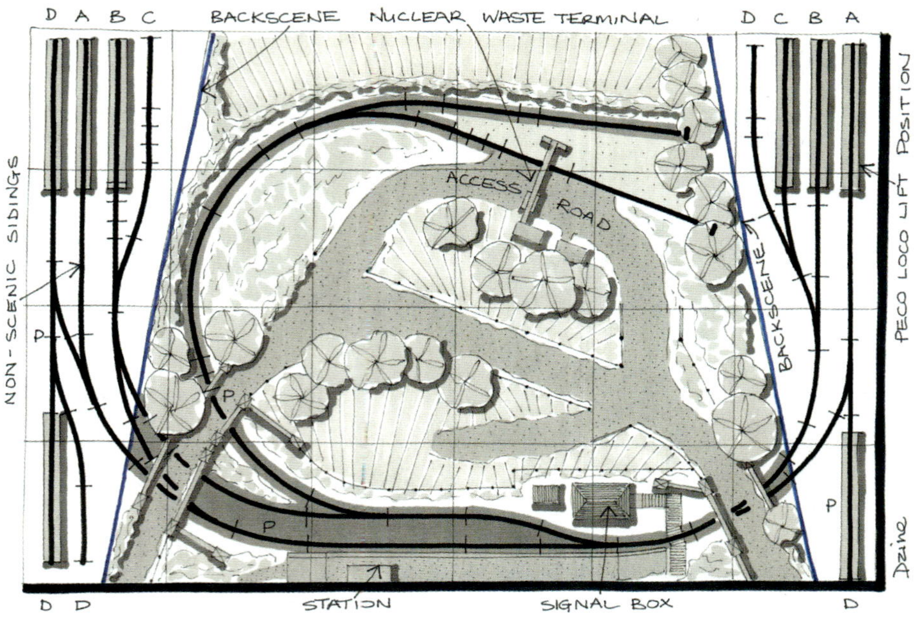

While compact for beginners, the design could easily be enlarged for those wanting a finer scale interpretation.

The section from Blaenau Ffestiniog to Llan Ffestiniog was originally a narrow gauge railway from 1868 and converted to standard gauge in 1883. Llan Ffestiniog to Bala opened in 1882 with the entire line consisting of many sharp check-railed curves over a steeply graded route. After closure of the Trawsfynydd to Bala section, part of the trackbed near Cwm Prysor was used for improving the A4212 and a further section, north of Frongoch, was flooded to create Llyn Celyn Reservoir. In the 1980s, explosives from Cooke's at Penrhyndeudraeth were handled out of Maentwrog Road goods yard and cement to the new power station also came in by rail. The last steam-hauled train was on January 22, 1961. Since full closure, there have been attempts to reopen part of the line as a heritage railway and while there have been complications, it seems the Bala & Ffestiniog Railway Heritage Trust are finally on track, no pun intended.

History and description at a glance

This simplified OO gauge Setrack entry-level plan combines the essence of Trawsfynydd nuclear waste sidings and a typical North Wales single platform halt in a minimum space of 6ft by 4ft. Note how the two sets of non-scenic sidings are almost a mirror image of each other with siding A for a two-car DMU or short nuclear waste train, siding B for a tank engine and solitary coach, siding C for a single railcar and siding D for loco holding (those with long enough straights can accommodate a Peco Loco Lift). All the curves are second radius and 'P' represents a power supply for those using DC. Scenically, the central area is roughly at bridge roadway height with a tree grouping forming a semi-view block between both sides of the layout.

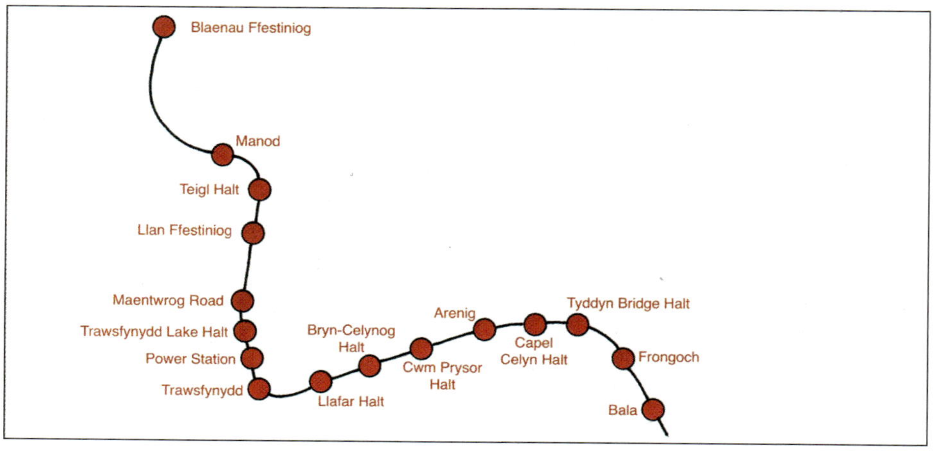

Location by location

ABOVE: The line originally commenced at **Blaenau Ffestiniog** GWR station, south of the current interchange station, squeezing between two modest retaining walls (also see the chapter covering Llandudno Junction to Blaenau Ffestiniog). On August 17, 1994, 31200 and 31201 with brake van B955125 and an out-of-sight nuclear waste train wait for a path to Llandudno Junction.

ABOVE, BELOW LEFT, BELOW RIGHT AND BOTTOM: **The line then snakes its way through the outskirts of town, passing between walls, under three bridges, over a level crossing and out towards Manod. 20903 with a weedkilling train consisting of three TTA tank wagons and four modified KCA Mk.1 coaches along with 20902 head out of Blaenau Ffestiniog to Trawsfynydd on August 25, 1994.**

LEFT: **Manod** replaced Tyddngwyn and was opened on September 10, 1883, before closing on April 2, 1917. It re-opened again on May 1, 1919, was reduced to halt status in 1955, closed to goods on January 1, 1960, and closed to passengers just over a year later. The main station building had a hipped roof and was a bungalow type structure, with flat-roofed toilet block and attached gable-ended section. A slate working incline at Craig Ddu fed to a nearby siding. The viaduct is of stone construction with brick arches and replaced the original timber trestle version, which was built when the line was narrow gauge.

Teigl Halt opened on September 14, 1931, and closed on January 4, 1960. It had a stockade platform infilled with ash and cinders, a pagoda shelter, oil lamp and occupation crossing at the southern end. There was a hut on the opposite side of the halt with phone and key apparatus to control access by a motor trolley. This was kept in a short siding south of the halt at 90 degrees to the main line. The trolley was lifted on and off the track by hand.

ABOVE: **Llan Ffestiniog** opened during 1882 and closed to passengers from January 4, 1960, and then completely 12 months later. The station consisted of a passing loop with two platforms and a pagoda shelter. There was a loading shed for slate, a yellow brick signal box with partial slate weatherboarding and a goods shed. The principal commodities included animal feed, coal, Morris Evans Oil, and tourist traffic to nearby Cynfall Falls.

Back in time 1

ABOVE AND RIGHT: **The route then weaves its way through some spectacular scenery to the outskirts of Maentwrog Road. The weedkilling train details are as in the earlier photos and 25167, which appears in all the black and white shots, dates from 1976.**

ABOVE, LEFT, OPPOSITE BELOW LEFT AND RIGHT: **This corner of the Fairbourne trackplan is fairly complex with its sector plate, sharp radius curves and diamond crossings. It is worth the effort to make this or have the track custom built. If not, consider altering the arrangement into something more entry-level.**

More modelling inspiration

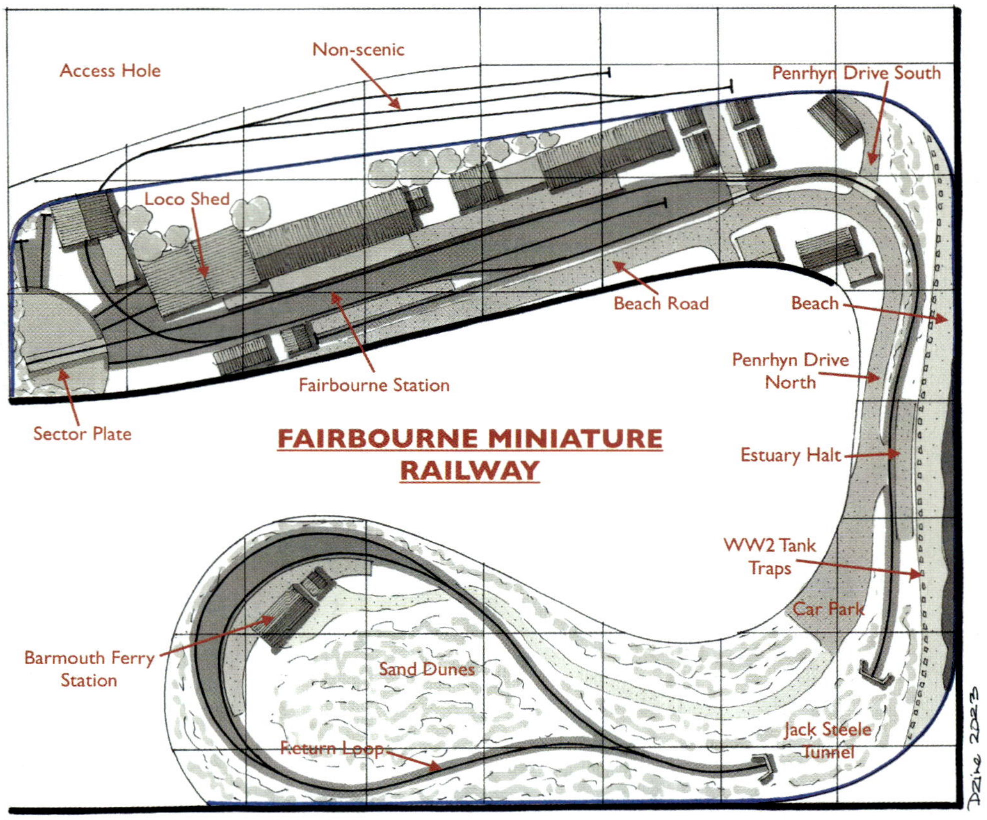

ABOVE: **With some adaptation to the Fairbourne-only plan shown here, you could model in either 009 or N. The 'U' shaped design employs prototypical curves near Beach Halt and north of Loop Halt and near the sea wall along the run to the tunnel. You will need to scratchbuild diamond crossings and curves near the loco shed or change the arrangement as on my previous plan. I imagine the non-scenic coach sidings to be automated but have also provided a small access hole for track cleaning.**

If you are looking for something scenically dynamic but occupying less length, why not consider Barmouth Ferry station to the nearest tunnel entrance, with a fiddle yard beyond. This could either be in a 'L' shaped format or straight along one wall.

Scale and gauge

Both accompanying trackplans look for easy solutions in terms of scale and gauge, but I just want to take a moment here to consider other options. If you model BR main line in O gauge (7mm/1ft) then the Fairbourne line, at roughly half-size, could be 009 (4mm/1ft) on 9mm N gauge track, representing 1ft 3in gauge. Alternately, if you model BR main line in OO (4mm/1ft) then the Fairbourne line, at half size, could be represented by N gauge (2mm/ft) with loco bodies on Z gauge mechanisms. In terms of Z gauge 6.5mm track, in OO this would represent a little over 1ft 6in and is nearer to the prototype's gauge for the pre-1985 period. Of course, the main issue is in adapting Z gauge mechanisms into N gauge loco bodies.

If neither of the above are to your taste, the only answer is to scratchbuild at least one or both of the two scales and if you are looking for a quick fix, do not include the BR section. For absolute scale/gauge accuracy, the key is in making sure that the Fairbourne track gauge of either 2ft, 15in or 12¼in is relevant for your chosen time period.

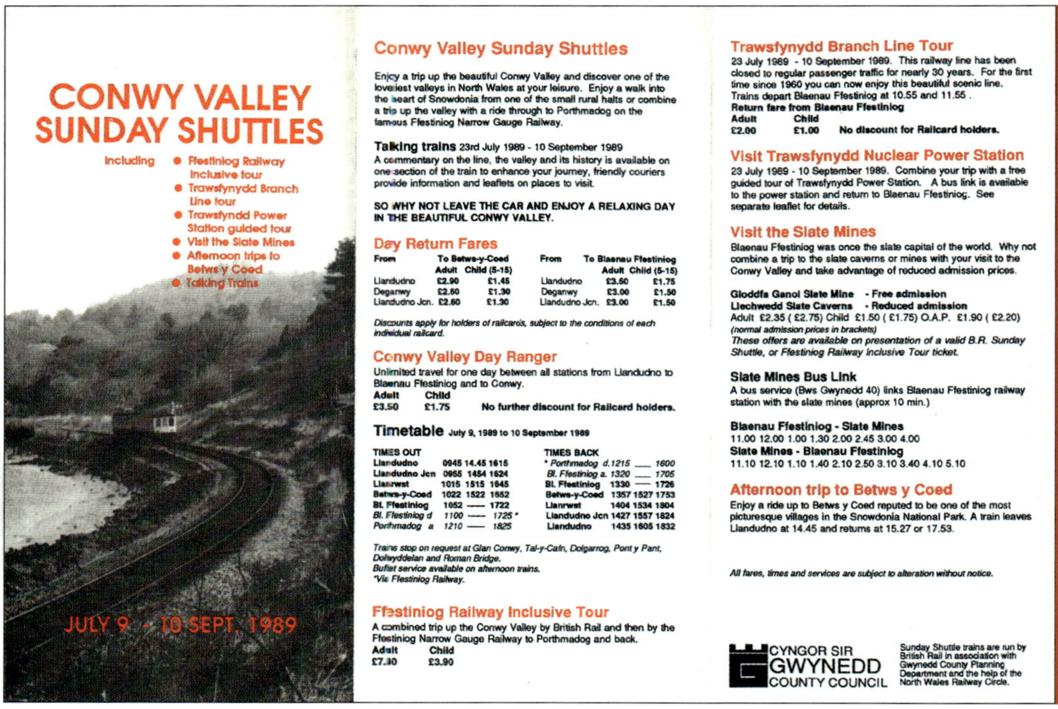

CONWY VALLEY SUNDAY SHUTTLES

Including
- Ffestiniog Railway Inclusive tour
- Trawsfynydd Branch Line tour
- Trawsfynydd Power Station guided tour
- Visit the Slate Mines
- Afternoon trips to Betws y Coed
- Talking Trains

JULY 9 - 10 SEPT. 1989

Conwy Valley Sunday Shuttles

Enjoy a trip up the beautiful Conwy Valley and discover one of the loveliest valleys in North Wales at your leisure. Enjoy a walk into the heart of Snowdonia from one of the small rural halts or combine a trip up the valley with a ride through to Porthmadog on the famous Ffestiniog Narrow Gauge Railway.

Talking trains 23rd July 1989 - 10 September 1989
A commentary on the line, the valley and its history is available on one section of the train to enhance your journey, friendly couriers provide information and leaflets on places to visit.

SO WHY NOT LEAVE THE CAR AND ENJOY A RELAXING DAY IN THE BEAUTIFUL CONWY VALLEY.

Day Return Fares

From	To Betws-y-Coed Adult	Child (5-15)	From	To Blaenau Ffestiniog Adult	Child (5-15)
Llandudno	£2.90	£1.45	Llandudno	£3.50	£1.75
Deganwy	£2.60	£1.30	Deganwy	£3.00	£1.50
Llandudno Jcn.	£2.60	£1.30	Llandudno Jcn.	£3.00	£1.50

Discounts apply for holders of railcards, subject to the conditions of each individual railcard.

Conwy Valley Day Ranger

Unlimited travel for one day between all stations from Llandudno to Blaenau Ffestiniog and to Conwy.

Adult £3.50 **Child** £1.75 **No further discount for Railcard holders.**

Timetable July 9, 1989 to 10 September 1989

TIMES OUT				TIMES BACK			
Llandudno	0945	14.45	1615	* *Porthmadog d.*	*1215*	—	*1600*
Llandudno Jcn	0955	1454	1624	*Bl. Ffestiniog a.*	*1320*	—	*1705*
Llanrwst	1015	1515	1645	Bl. Ffestiniog	1330	—	1726
Betws-y-Coed	1022	1522	1652	Betws-y-Coed	1357	1527	1753
Bl. Ffestiniog	1052	—	1722	Llanrwst	1404	1534	1804
Bl. Ffestiniog d	*1100*	—	*1725 **	Llandudno Jcn	1427	1557	1824
Porthmadog a	*1210*	—	*1825*	Llandudno	1435	1605	1832

Trains stop on request at Glan Conwy, Tal-y-Cafn, Dolgarrog, Pont y Pant, Dolwyddelan and Roman Bridge.
Buffet service available on afternoon trains.
**Via Ffestiniog Railway.*

Ffestiniog Railway Inclusive Tour

A combined trip up the Conwy Valley by British Rail and then by the Ffestiniog Narrow Gauge Railway to Porthmadog and back.

Adult £7.[illegible]0 **Child** £3.90

Trawsfynydd Branch Line Tour

23 July 1989 - 10 September 1989. This railway line has been closed to regular passenger traffic for nearly 30 years. For the first time since 1960 you can now enjoy this beautiful scenic line. Trains depart Blaenau Ffestiniog at 10.55 and 11.55 .

Return fare from Blaenau Ffestiniog
Adult £2.00 **Child** £1.00 **No discount for Railcard holders.**

Visit Trawsfynydd Nuclear Power Station

23 July 1989 - 10 September 1989. Combine your trip with a free guided tour of Trawsfynydd Power Station. A bus link is available to the power station and return to Blaenau Ffestiniog. See separate leaflet for details.

Visit the Slate Mines

Blaenau Ffestiniog was once the slate capital of the world. Why not combine a trip to the slate caverns or mines with your visit to the Conwy Valley and take advantage of reduced admission prices.

Gloddfa Ganol Slate Mine - **Free admission**
Llechwedd Slate Caverns - **Reduced admission**
Adult £2.35 (£2.75) Child £1.50 (£1.75) O.A.P. £1.90 (£2.20)
(normal admission prices in brackets)
These offers are available on presentation of a valid B.R. Sunday Shuttle, or Ffestiniog Railway Inclusive Tour ticket.

Slate Mines Bus Link
A bus service (Bws Gwynedd 40) links Blaenau Ffestiniog railway station with the slate mines (approx 10 min.)

Blaenau Ffestiniog - Slate Mines
11.00 12.00 1.00 1.30 2.00 2.45 3.00 4.00
Slate Mines - Blaenau Ffestiniog
11.10 12.10 1.10 1.40 2.10 2.50 3.10 3.40 4.10 5.10

Afternoon trip to Betws y Coed

Enjoy a ride up to Betws y Coed reputed to be one of the most picturesque villages in the Snowdonia National Park. A train leaves Llandudno at 14.45 and returns at 15.27 or 17.53.

All fares, times and services are subject to alteration without notice.

CYNGOR SIR GWYNEDD COUNTY COUNCIL

Sunday Shuttle trains are run by British Rail in association with Gwynedd County Planning Department and the help of the North Wales Railway Circle.

ABOVE LEFT, ABOVE RIGHT AND LEFT: **Maentwrog Road** opened on November 1, 1882, closing to passengers on January 4, 1960, and to freight (except for through traffic) in January 1961, It then re-opened for a Sundays-only service from a temporary platform covering the goods yard siding on May 21, 1989. There was a service the following year but to ride the line only. In earlier times, regular traffic included that from a tannery at nearby Gellilydan.

Trawsfynydd Lake Halt opened in 1934 and was aimed at those who fish or walk. It consisted of a 50ft long wooden stockade platform filled with ash and cinders, complete with a shelter and oil lamp.

Back in time 2

ABOVE AND OPPOSITE BOTTOM: **Trawsfynydd Power Station** was constructed in 1959. It became operational in 1965 and closed during 1991, although it has since been redeveloped as small scale reactors. The substantial structure was designed by Basil Spence. There were two sidings but no run-round loop, so trains reversed here, or were top and tailed, all the way from Blaenau Ffestiniog. Several different types of nuclear flask wagon were used and two are seen here; in the colour photo are FNAs from Lot 4063 built by Procor between 1988-89. The black and white photo is a Flatrol MJ from Lot 3300, which was built at Swindon and modified by BREL (cradle and Y25 bogies). 31201 and 31200 appearing in the later photos are from August 1994 whereas those of 25167 date back to 1976.

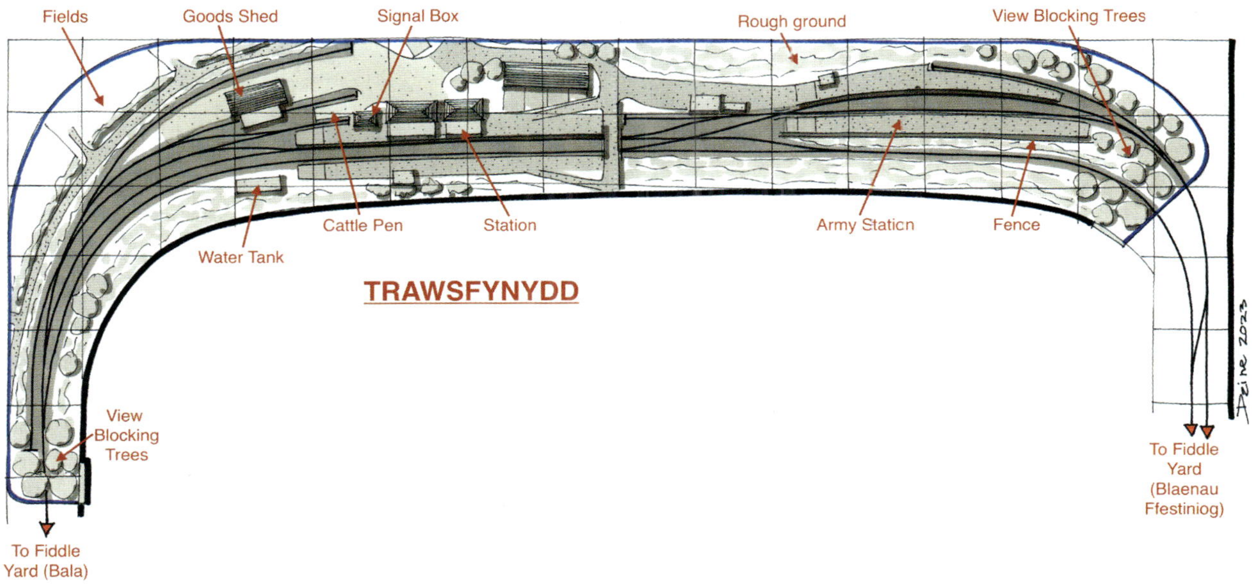

ABOVE: **Trawsfynydd** had two stations, one for the public and the other for army use. The latter originally served a camp at Golau but was superseded by a larger version at Bronaber, near Rhiw Goch. It was used mainly for ammunition, guns, men, and horses. An unusual detailing feature was the wooden fence between the station and main line to avoid unsettling the horses. Prisoners of both wars were kept here, and traffic reduced in 1945, closing in the 1950s, only to be re-opened to house the workforce for the new power station. The accompanying OO gauge trackplan is designed to fit in a standard 16ft by 8ft garage and is an oval layout with a lengthy fiddle yard, not shown, on the opposite side. Those with insufficient space may wish to go down to N gauge at 8ft long but with a 5ft width in order to create sufficient space for a central operating well.

Llafar halt opened on March 1, 1932, and closed on January 4, 1960, to passengers and completely from January 28, 1961. It was similar in layout to Trawsfynydd Lake and with a corrugated pagoda-style shelter.

Bryn-Celynog Halt was opened on March 13, 1939, and also closed in January 1960. The platform was again similar to Trawsfynydd Lake.

TOP LEFT AND TOP RIGHT, ABOVE AND RIGHT: **Cwm Prysor Halt** was at the line's summit, 1,278ft above sea level. Originally single track, a passing loop was added in 1906 and then removed in 1951. The halt consisted of a brick-faced platform and wooden pent waiting room with ornate front fascia, sign and two gas lamps. Note the station house, still extant, is situated near where a ground frame and level crossing with wicket gates once existed and there was a hut at the opposite end. While this 10ft by 8ft OO gauge layout has a solitary scenic loop, it has been designed for those who prefer seeing trains traverse their way through dramatic scenery. As such, there is a need for some substantial baseboard construction for the lower level lake, viaduct and hillside track 'shelf' between the viaduct and fiddle yard. The latter has quite short loops but are long enough to handle prototype length trains.

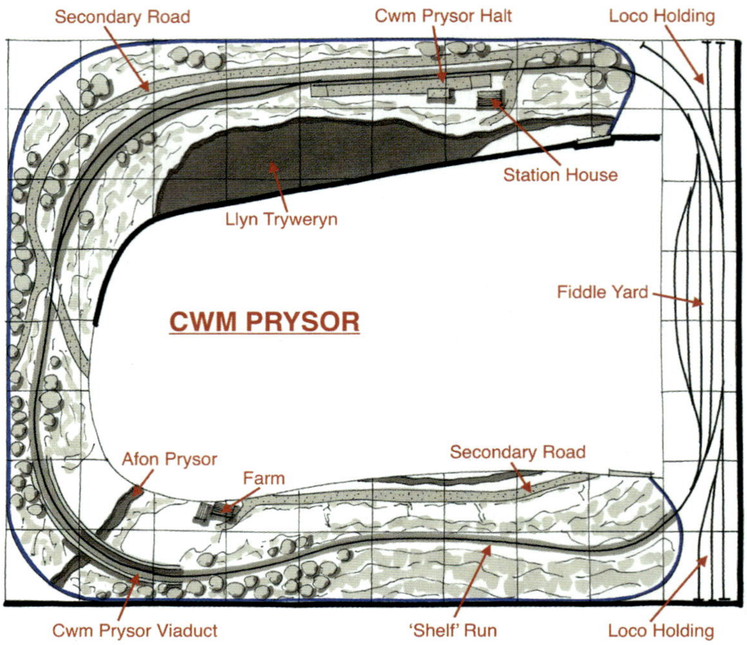

ABOVE LEFT AND ABOVE RIGHT: **Cwm Prysor Viaduct** consists of nine 36ft wide brick arches with stone piers and is approximately 105ft (42cm in OO) above the stream below and 490ft long (1.96 metres in OO) and will undoubtedly need some compression to fit the space. The track was on a sharp curve with check rail. Repair work in 1953 saw the parapet wall raised and metal railings added.

Arenig opened on November 1, 1882, mirroring the other stations in closing to passengers from the start of 1960 and then completely a year later. A nearby granite quarry mainly provided crushed stone for railway ballast. The stone crusher was next to the line with a conveyor over the station. The conveyor replaced a narrow gauge railway and was installed in 1940. There was a signal box on the Blaenau platform and a waiting shelter on the other. A GWR water column was also provided.

Capel Celyn Halt opened on December 1, 1930, and closed from January 4, 1960. It was on the north side of a horseshoe bend with a single curved 70ft-long platform; this being a wooden stockade backfilled with ash and cinders, with an elliptical-roofed corrugated shelter and two oil lamps.

Tyddyn Bridge Halt opened on the first day of 1930 and closed 30 years later. The platform was a wooden construction with an elliptical roof corrugated shelter and two oil lamps. There was a rail bridge at one end and a road overbridge at the other. The line crossed the Afon Tryweryn site and is now buried under Lyn Celyn Dam wall.

Frongoch opened from November 1, 1882, closed to passengers on January 4, 1960, and closed completely on January 28, 1961. There was a single platform along with a siding to a goods shed and cattle pens. Some buildings have survived, including the platform-mounted signal box. There was a prisoner of war camp nearby and this was a source of traffic.

RIGHT, BELOW LEFT AND BELOW RIGHT: **Bala opened on November 1, 1882, and closed from January 18, 1965. There was a goods shed that resembled a castle with mock battlements and turrets, a small engine shed south east of the station, two platforms, a signal box, and a steel footbridge. All three accompanying photos show 41241 on the Bala Junction service on August 29, 1964.** Richard Inwood/Paul A Lunn Collection

Simplified Setrack

Here we have another entry-level 6ft by 4ft layout based on several key components; a modified version of Maentwrog Road station and yard, Trawsfynydd nuclear waste sidings, and Blaenau Ffestiniog's slate spoil heap. The layout works well as a self-contained unit for two trains; a two-car DMU and a Class 24 or 25 freight (nuclear waste and gunpowder). With two loops capable of holding at least the DMU, there is plenty of opportunity for shunting. If you want just that little bit more, then having already factored in an extension curve at bottom right, you can add a non-scenic fiddle yard. I have kept mine small at 4ft but, if you have got a bit more space, then take advantage with a three-car DMU or longer freight.

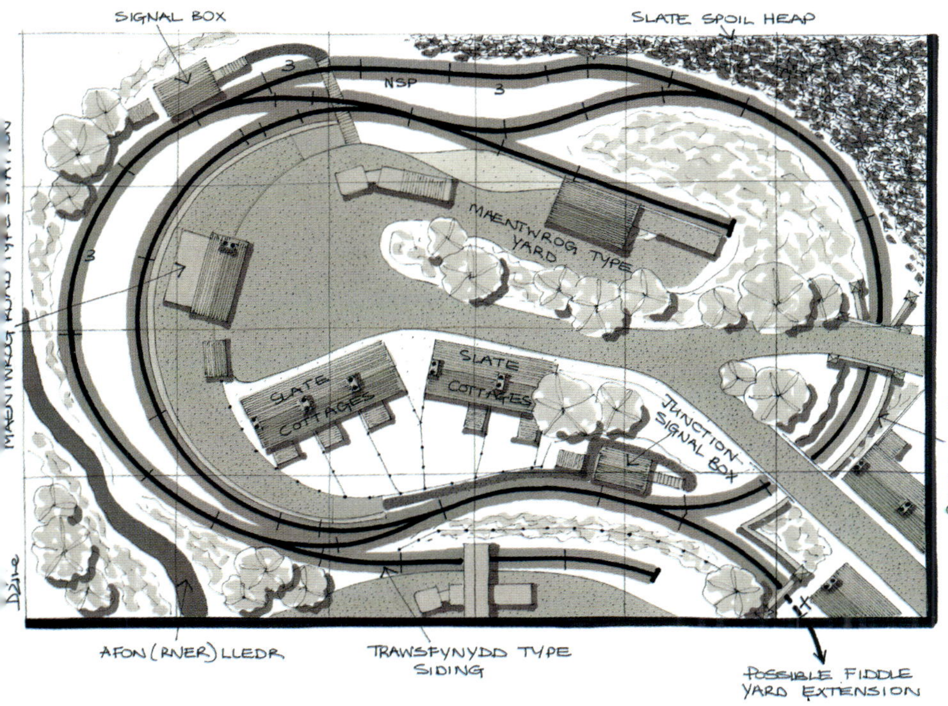

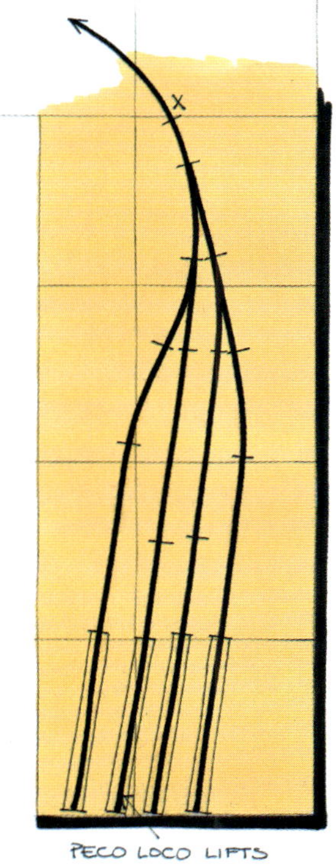

Locos and stock

0-4-2T and 0-6-0T locos were the mainstay and included the following classes: 2251, 43xx (military trains only), 5700 and 7400. Actual locos known to have appeared are 3749 and 4645. Most passenger trains were one or two coaches or mixed with freight.

Dyserth branch

History and description at a glance

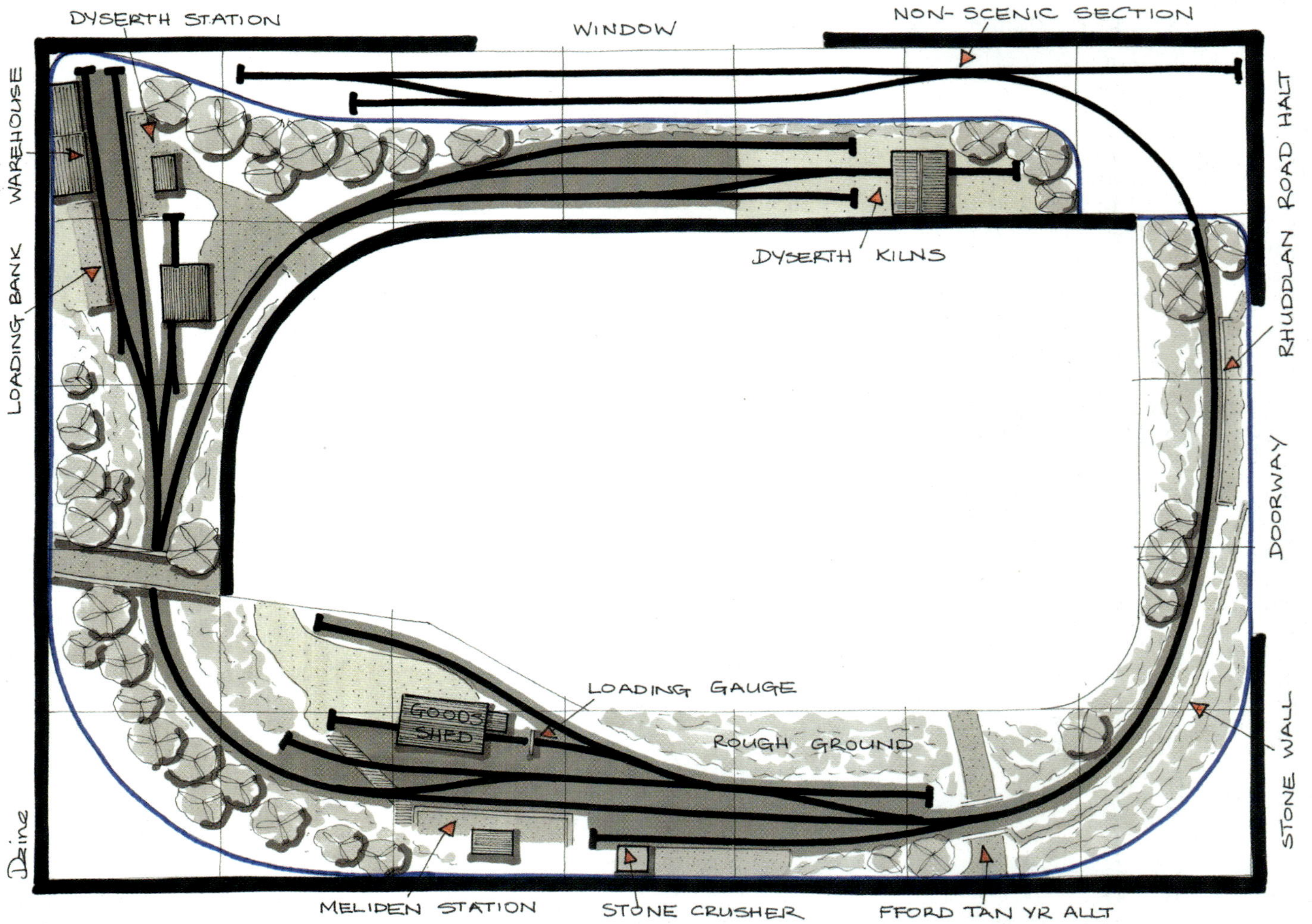

ABOVE: **A 7ft by 5ft OO gauge layout suitable for a small garden shed or spare room. Oval in appearance, it is in fact a wrapped round end-to-end design. With largely one coach length platforms, I have been able to pack in three stations without looking overcrowded and there is plenty of shunting opportunity at the two stations of Meliden and Dyserth along with the kilns.**

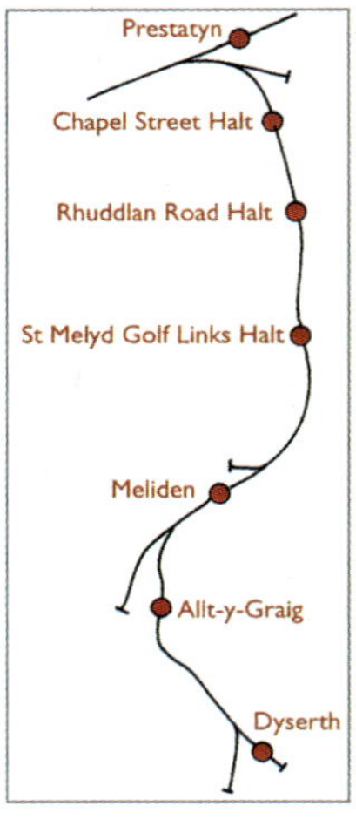

LEFT: **Opened in 1869, a regular passenger service commenced from August 28, 1905, but was withdrawn from September 22, 1930. Stone carrying trains continued until September 5, 1973. A 2.5 mile long branch from Prestatyn's coastal plains to the Clwydian Range, it was steeply graded with many a sharp curve. Goods traffic included lead and haematite (used in paints, jewellery, radiation shields and polishing), agricultural products and household coal. It was popular with tourists due to Dyserth Castle ruins and Cwm waterfalls, near Dyserth, and there was a very frequent service, often more than the timetable suggested!**

Location by location

ABOVE: **Dyserth station.** After passing under a large bridge, linking two fields on the outskirts, the line splits in two from a single track 'Y' junction; west over Afon Ffyddon to the kilns, which closed in September 1973, and east to the station, which featured a platform (served from Newmarket Road), goods shed, loading bank and warehouse. Dyserth goods shed had a footprint of 32ft by 26ft with the yard having similar facilities to Meliden. Additionally, the station platform was roughly in front of the shed, centre left, with a livestock pen at the end of the loading bay.

Allt-y-Graig opened on February 1, 1929, and was situated between Meliden and Dyserth. It had a brief life, closing on September 22, 1930.

ABOVE: Vale of Clwyd Farmers buildings (right), goods traffic ended in May 1964 with parcel facilities withdrawn from December 1957.

ABOVE: A railmotor with trailer car departs Meliden station on its way to Dyserth.

ABOVE: **Meliden station** was comprised of a loop, ground level station platform, loading platform and stone crusher, coal siding, extant goods shed (now a visitor centre) and branch to Talargdch Mine Main Works. Meliden goods shed had an original 50ft by 30ft footprint with an additional 16ft square office. There were sidings used for a quartet of coal wharves and general goods, but they were closed by April 1957.

St. Melyd Golf Links Halt opened 1923, the line then curving towards Ffordd Tan Yr Allt and passing Talargdch Mine East Works and Mostyn Engine Shaft.

ABOVE: Rhuddlan Road Halt was re-named **Woodland Park** in 1923 and was long enough for one coach. It featured a low-level gravelled platform contained within what looks like railway sleepers. There are two lamps on posts of different heights, a station name sign and, beyond the far platform end, another sign, possibly about trespassing, although it is hard to tell.

Chapel Street Halt opened from January 21, 1906. It was sometimes referred to as Prestatyn Chapel Street, being on the edge of the town. There was a level crossing nearby dating from the 1950s. The halt closed on September 22, 1930.

Prestatyn station was a short journey along the main line and accessed from a kick-back headshunt, where railmotors reversed on and off the branch. There was a gasworks siding off the branch, which was operational until the 1960s. Prestatyn No.2 box controlled access to the Dyserth branch, this originally having 30 levers, which later grew to 45 after the closure of No.1 box. The No.2 box, now preserved, is situated near the end of platform one, a bay siding. It has a brick base locking room and timber operating room. Up to 1920, there was a low-level platform serving the Dyserth branch at the western end of platform one with a fence to protect passengers from passing main line trains. After 1920, railmotors were replaced with push-pull locos and carriages. The track in the bay platform was removed in 1980.

Locos and stock

ABOVE LEFT AND ABOVE RIGHT: London and North Western railmotors traversed the branch from 1905 to 1930 and therefore define the operational period. While there are no models available ready-to-run in OO gauge, a 3D printed version is available from Shapeways by Simon Dawson at Recreation21. If you want to cram more into your available space, there are N and HO versions too, which Simon advises he powered by using a stripped down Dapol or Hornby Pug. While not on the branch, the accompanying postcards show both sides and interior of a Dyserth unit.

After railmotors, LNWR push-pull trains operated to the end of passenger services. LMS 4Fs and BR (ex-LMS) Class 5s were regular on the line and Class 24/ 25 diesels in later BR days. There were specials, including a tank engine and three coaches along with DMUs. Due to the absence of a run-round loop at Dyserth, all loco-hauled stock reversed along the branch at 15mph!

More modelling inspiration

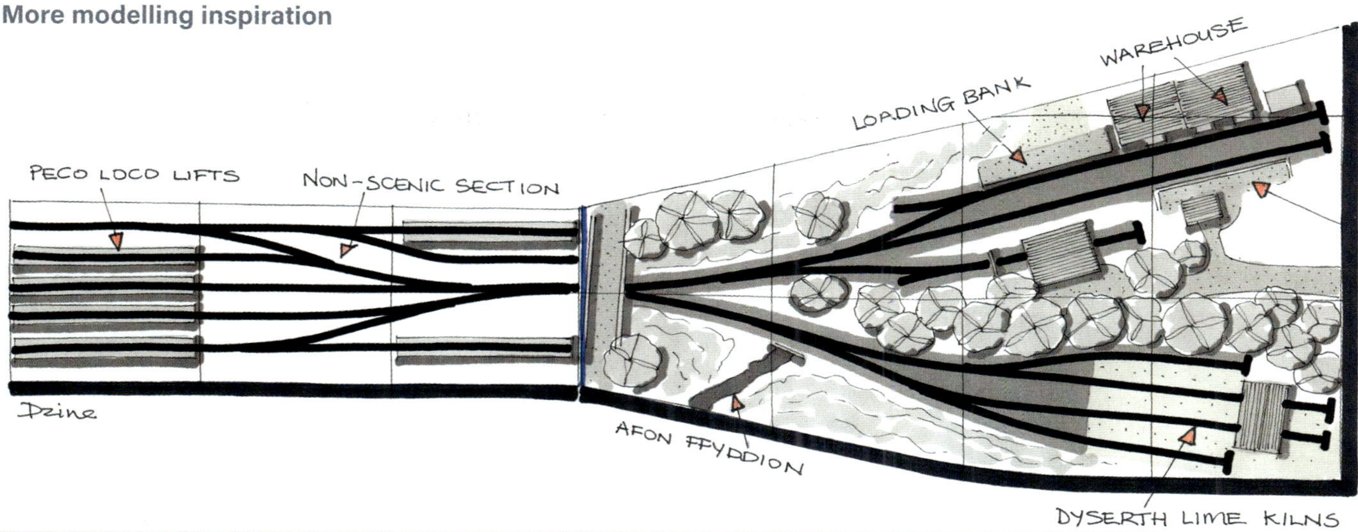

ABOVE: This contrasting OO gauge end-to-end design is 7ft by 2ft 6in and is semi-fictitious. It compresses the station, goods yard, and kilns together with a partial row of view-blocking trees between the two. The fiddle yard makes use of Peco Loco-Lifts and potential positions are shown on plan. Devoid of any scenic run-round loop, I anticipate trains will be either propelled into sidings or a shunter will be used to release any trapped loco. While a self-contained unit, I imagine this layout to be built in two sections; scenic and fiddle yard, so that future expansion could include other locations in 'L' or 'U' format.

Simplified Setrack

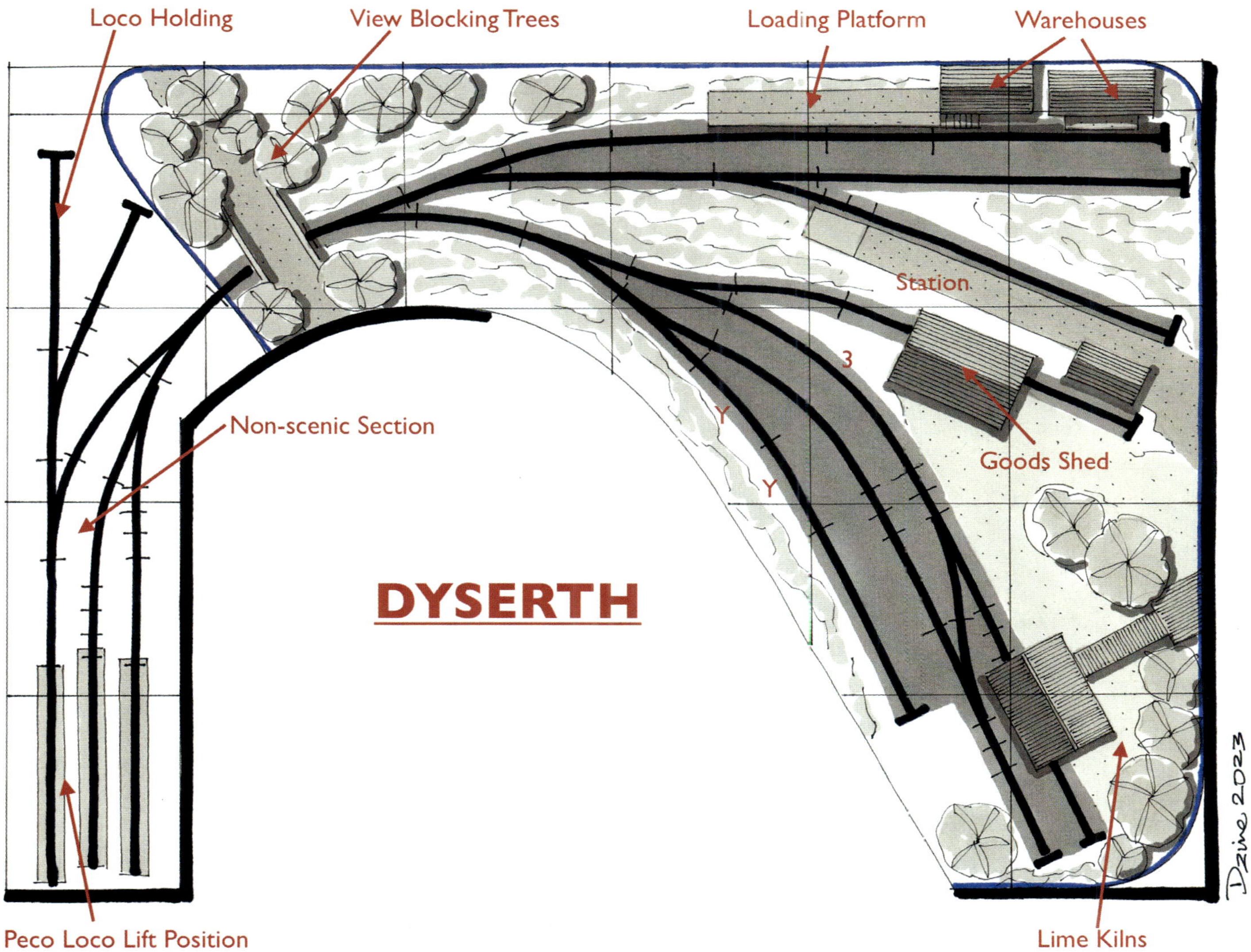

ABOVE: While intensely compressed, all the main prototype terminus components are included in this OO gauge 6ft by 4ft 3in layout. There is plenty of shunting to be had and with little change in appearance over the years, it would be possible to operate different time periods. A fictious passenger service in the diesel era could be operated using a single-car DMU.

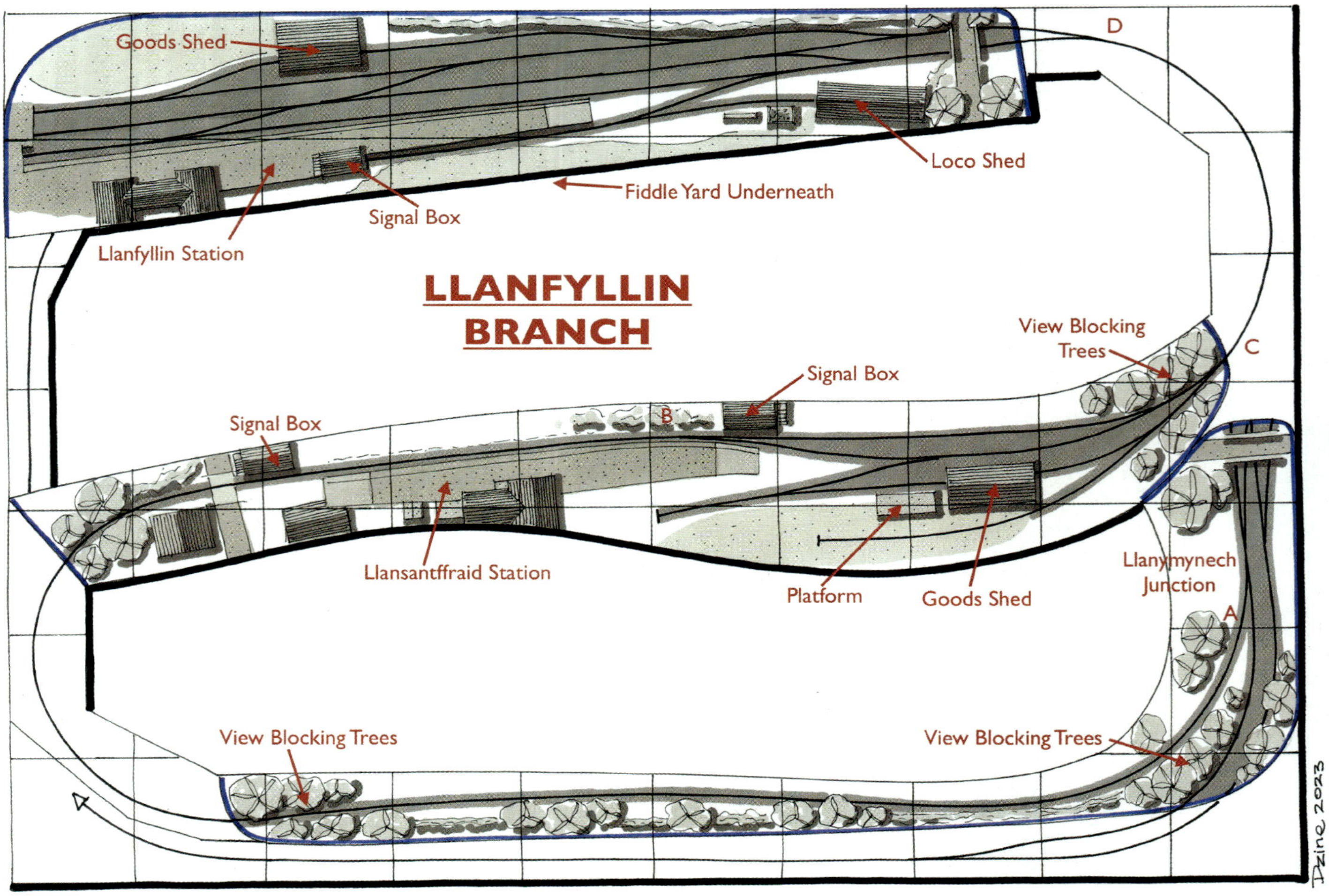

Llanfyllin branch

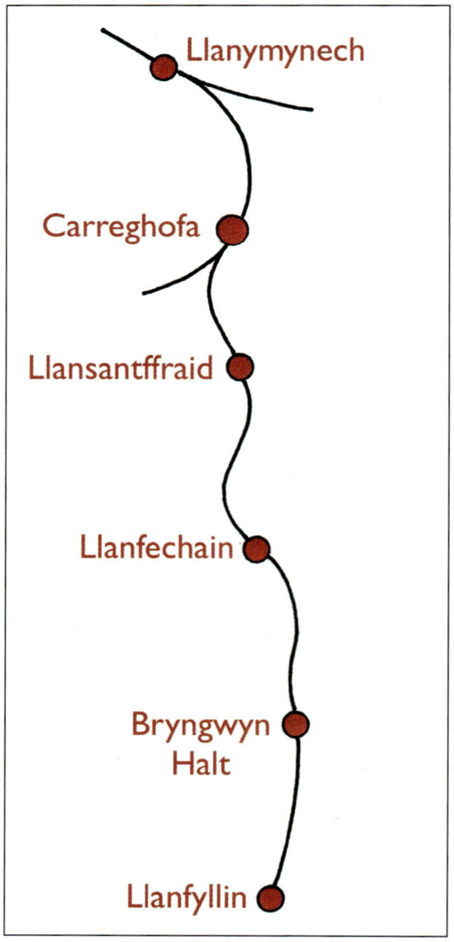

History and description at a glance

This OO gauge branch layout consists of two stations, a scenic run, junction, and fiddle yard in a space of 10ft by 7ft. The terminus at Llanfyllin has almost all straight track except for one siding and a turntable, the latter omitted to keep the baseboard width to a minimum. The main compromise is that on each end of the Llansantffraid station baseboard section, I have orientated the track opposite to the prototype. There are two solutions to this, increase the baseboard length to about 14ft, or replace it with the less physically demanding Llanfechain station, this easily fitting into 10ft. The scenic run provides opportunity for some impressive work and the junction and bridge at Llanymynech prototypically view blocks the main line in one direction, while the other has a fictitious tree grouping. The substantial task with this design is that 19ft of the run, from A to B and C to D, needs to be on a 1:40 gradient, providing clearance of just over 4ft at Llanymynech Junction and 5ft 5in between Llanfyllin terminus and the fiddle yard below. A gradient pf 1:35 will give 6ft clearance at the latter and should be fine for the short trains used on the line.

The branch was accessed from Llanymynech and traversed an east-west route initially along the River Vyrnwy Valley. There is an excellent, if somewhat dark, silent colour film from January 1965 which is part of the British Film Institute collection (www.player.bfi.org.uk). Much of it can be used as a point of reference, especially for those rarely modelled details and for more accurate colouring. Now for the bad news, it covers only four stations, excluding Llanfyllin, and several sequences have not been filmed/edited in the correct geographic order.

Location by location

ABOVE: **Llanfyllin station** opened on July 17, 1863, and closed 102 years later. It consisted of a brick-built station and large goods shed with recessed panels, along with a loco shed, single platform with Cambrian Railway signal box and overbridge. The line was built to serve the limestone quarries along the Llanfyllin Valley. There must have been some level of tourism as a camping coach was situated there in 1939. Richard Inwood/Paul A Lunn Collection

Bryngwyn, originally Brongwyn, opened in 1863 and was re-named Bryngwyn Halt from 1923; closure coming on January 18, 1965. It featured a Pent corrugated iron shelter in later life, mounted on a narrow, timber trestle, slabbed platform with a concrete post, tube and wire fence, and a couple of oil lamps. The whole structure was on an embankment, situated on the west side of the B4393 Llanfechain Road bridge, with stepped access between the two. In all, a pleasant modelling composition.

ABOVE: **Llanfechain station** was opened in January 1866 and closed in 1965. The station house and station with shelter combined were constructed from brick with stone sills and lintels. A stone bridge stood nearby at the Llanfyllin end, while there was initially a six-lever ground frame until the late 1920s. This was reduced in size until the yard closed on July 27, 1964.

ABOVE: **Llansantffraid station** was originally known as Llansaintffraid at least until the early 1900s. Opened in 1863 and closed 1965, it encompassed a single platform with brick-built station building, goods shed, warehouse, cattle dock, two Dutton and Co. Cambrian Railway signal boxes, a level crossing, Kempster's warehouse and siding, and Wynnstay Farmers Mill nearby. Some of the site is still intact.

Carreghofa Halt was opened on April 11, 1938, and closed from January 18, 1965. The line here, near the B4398, had originally been part of the Nantmawr branch, with a new section of line added to avoid Llanfyllin branch trains reversing. The halt employed a timber waiting shelter and timber stockade platform front, backfilled with a top layer of chippings, along with a post and tube fence and a ramp from the station to the road. The structure was set in a modest cutting on a slight curve, and adjacent to a pair of bridges side by side; these being a stone arch and plate girder. There was also a platelayer's hut at the opposite end.

ABOVE LEFT AND ABOVE RIGHT: **Llanymynech Junction. The accompanying two photos shows the last straight section of track and curve into the junction at Llanymynech. The location of the B4398 bridge at the southern end of Llanymynech station means intending modellers that want to represent part of the main line do not have to include the station, especially if space is tight.** Richard Inwood/Paul A Lunn Collection

Locos used on the branch included Dean Goods, 14xx, Ivatt Class 2, especially 46503, 46527 and 46512. The latter was a regular and hauled a SLS special on January 17, 1965.

Simplified Setrack

As you can see in the larger track plan, the original layout at Llanfyllin is extremely long and, as such, I have heavily compressed it to fit a space of 6ft 6in by 8ft. This includes a fiddle yard, although it is not shown on the plan for this OO gauge entry-level version. The most noticeable absences are the second loop between the bridge and goods yard and the turntable. On the plus side, pretty much everything else is replicated as per the real place. I have avoided a backscene at the left-hand end, so you can see down the line's entire length, this making up for the partial front view blocking by the substantial station building. If you are wanting a minimum space layout then Carreghofa Halt, with its unusual and rarely modelled pair of bridges within touching distance of each other, stands out from the run-of-the-mill.

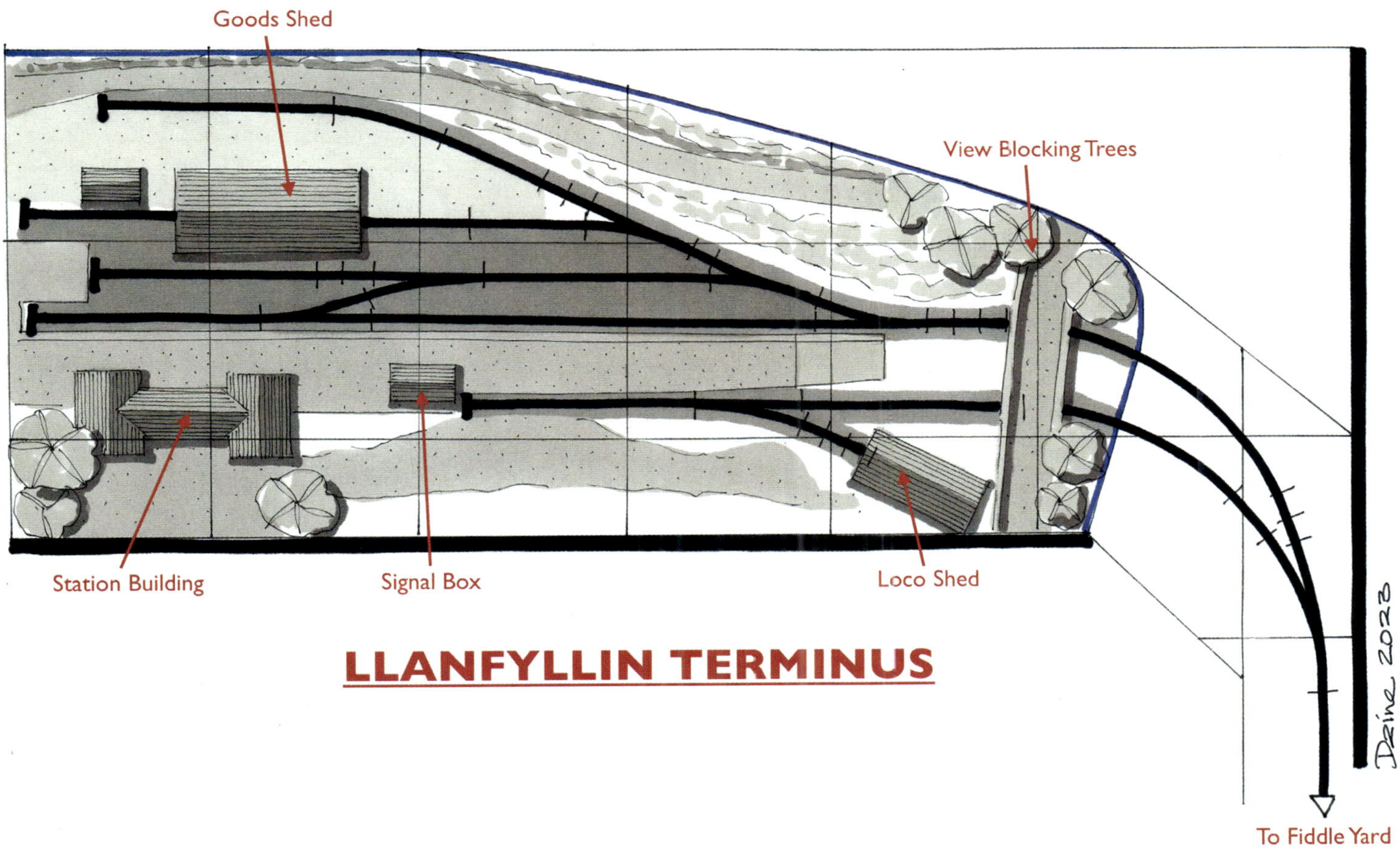

The Van branch

History and description at a glance

I include this pair of images of a N gauge inglenook to show how prototype and fictional features can be manipulated into an improved arrangement. Please note the main backscene is behind the trees and the end backscene is situated behind the added row of fictional cottages. In all other respects, it looks just like the real place with the loco shed no longer connected to the rail network. The second 3D, with the exact same Inglenook trackplan, has everything juxtaposed; the loco shed is now on part of the operational layout and the station is easier to view from the front baseboard edge, while still having the feel of Caersws.

The accompanying 7ft by 5ft layout plan is circa 1900 and incorporates both termini in fairly accurate if somewhat shorter than prototype length. The left-hand end curve is a fictitious device to make the almost oval format work, adding a kick-back fiddle yard with accessing headshunt. I would not want to go much smaller than this in OO gauge and indeed a little extra length would help extend the run from Caersws station throat and Afon Carno bridge on one side and the siding length at Van Mine on the other.

The Van Railway opened on August 14, 1871. Productivity at the mine peaked in 1877 with nearly 6,500 tons of lead and 2,400 tons of zinc extracted along with a quantity of silver. Numerous other mines sprung up to work the Van Lode as it was found to be an extremely rich seam. In addition to moving the spoils, the railway offered a short-lived passenger service between 1873 and 1879. Mining ceased in 1893 and the line closed, re-opening three years later after agreement with the Cambrian Railway. The former mines provided a source for railway ballast and, after another temporary closure between 1920-23, the GWR re-activated and operated the line until final closure in 1940.

There were two stations at Caersws, the lesser known being built just after a junction with the Cambrian main line. It featured a loop and two sidings, one of which served a modest brick-built loco shed, which was closed in 1893 and re-opened by the Cambrian in 1896 before finally closing in 1922, although it continued in use as a railway engineering workshop, certainly into the 1970s.

Set in the Cerist and Trannon river valleys, the 6.5-mile branch from Van to Caersws is almost straight throughout, passing through a lightly populated, gently rolling, and pleasant landscape. There is an excellent book entitled *Northern Mines Research Society, British Mining No.31, The Van Mines* by Nigel A. Chapman (ISBN 9780901450616) containing several railway images and

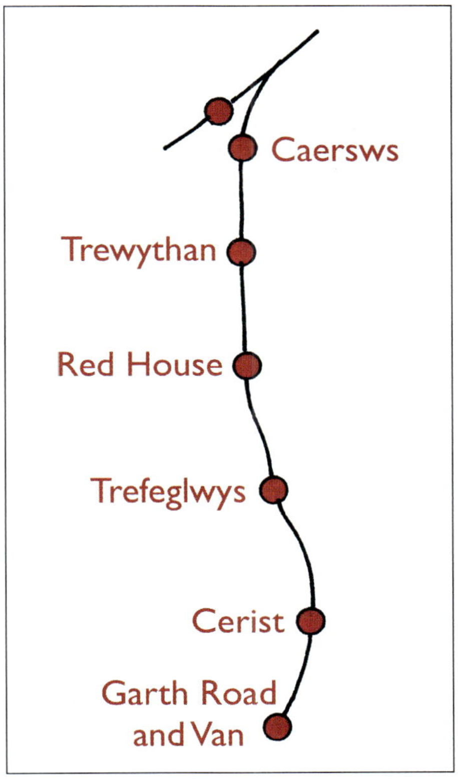

relevant information. New and sometimes second-hand copies are available from The Northern Mine Research Society (www.nmrs.org.uk).

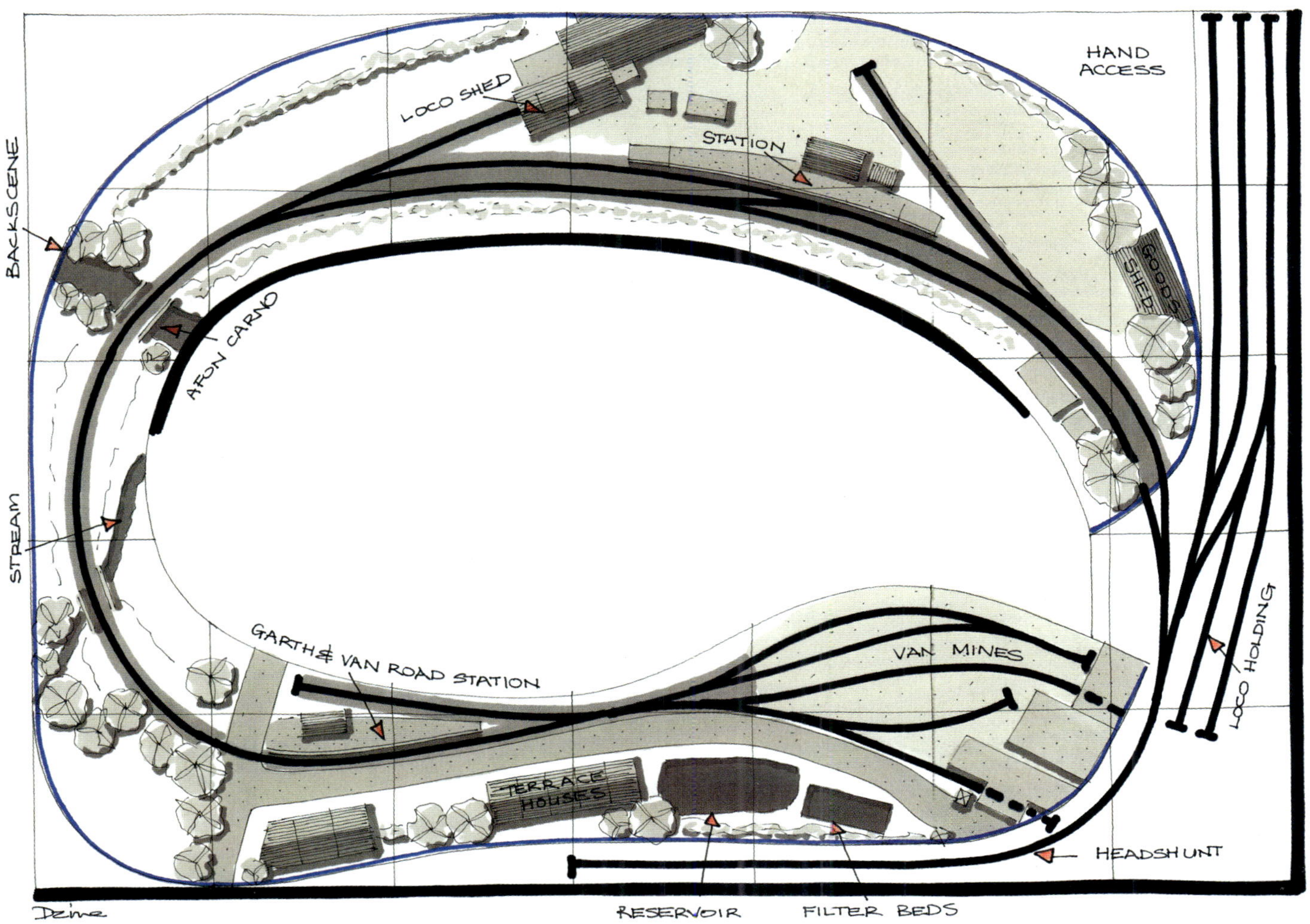

Location by location

BELOW: **Garth Road and Van (Y Fan) opened from December 1, 1873, and closed in July 1879, while goods traffic ceased on November 1, 1940. It served the village of Garth, near the current Van Institute building. Services included excursions and school children, even after closure to passengers.**

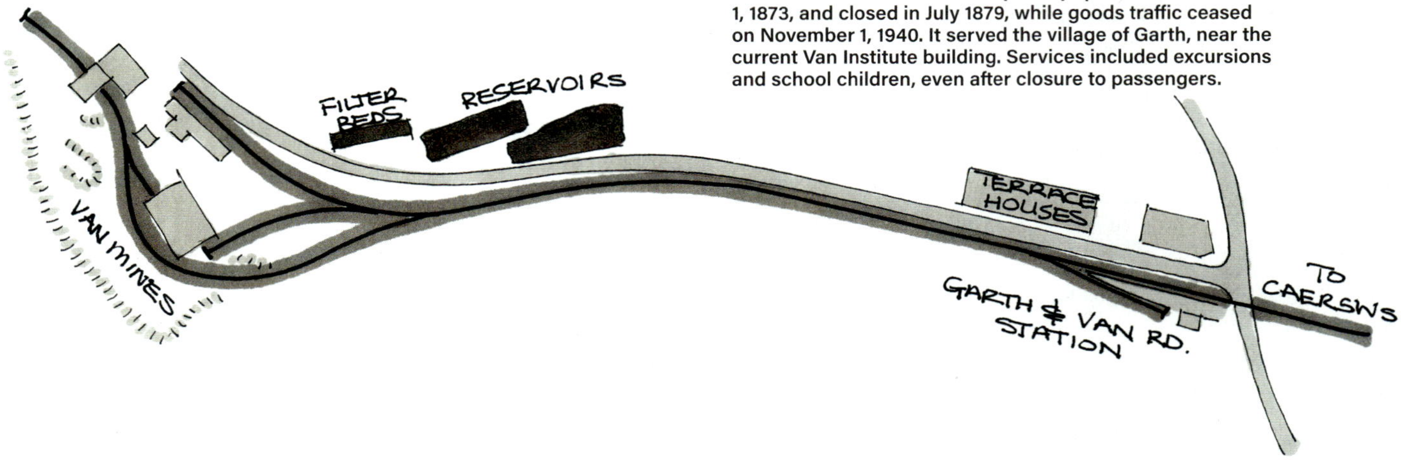

Cerist also opened at the start of December 1873, closure coming on November 4, 1940. This was a request stop with a solitary siding. The B4569 crossed the line by a stone overbridge and the parapets still exist.

Of the other stations, **Trefeglwys** was near a level crossing on Stokes Lane, Pwll-glas, while **Red House** served the nearby village to the south of the line. **Trewythan** was the first station out of Caersws and served the village, also located slightly south of the line and only a short distance from Red House.

LEFT AND BELOW: **Caersws consisted of a main station building in red brick with a slate roof. There are two windows with a door between, slightly offset to the left in the front elevation. Adjacent, there is a concrete store, door to the left and one window in the front elevation and a corrugated roof. A little distance away is a medium-sizes, pre-fabricated Provender store. Lastly, an extant loco shed, constructed from Yellow brick, English Bond, with a slate roof, offset louvered vent nearer the Van end and 16 paned cast iron ornate windows on stone sills. The loco doors are offset to the left-hand side when facing the ex-Cambrian main line. Please note all structures, while listed buildings, are now contained within a builder's yard.**

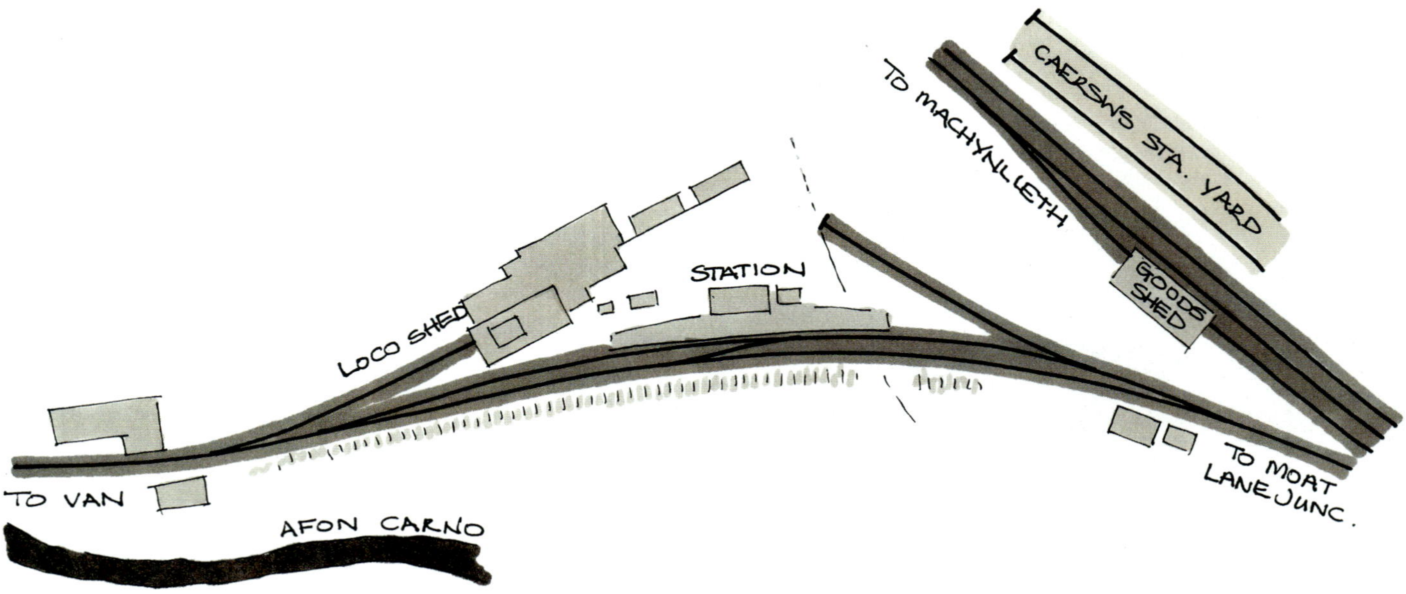

RIGHT: **Caersws Junction.** A medium-sized stone and slate roofed goods shed, perfectly positioned to view block access to a 'main line' fiddle yard. The junction was controlled from an 18-lever Dutton & Co. type 1 box, this having a brick base with timber operating room and corner chimney. The cabin survived into the 1990s to control the nearby level crossing.

Locos

The Manning Wardle locos could be represented by modifying a Hornby Peckett, although there are a number of 3D printed bodies available to fit their ubiquitous 0-4-0 chassis. It was also worked by a pair of old Class I 0-6-0Ts, later renamed K Class, Nos. 374 and 668. These were of 1870s vintage and are available as metal kits from RT Models (www.rtmodels.co.uk). Although associated with the Dinas Mawddwy branch, GWR 0-6-0T Manning Wardle No. 824, formerly Cambrian Railway No. 30, spent some of its later life on the Van Branch before withdrawal in 1940. With Machynlleth loco shed just over 20 miles away, you could add variety from its allocation of GWR locos, especially smaller classes like Pannier tanks, Dukedogs and Dean Goods.

Simplified Setrack

This Caersws-only 6ft by 4ft 6in layout for OO gauge is a straightforward oval with central operating well. I have included a substantial non-scenic section with passing loop, large enough for the longest anticipated train, a siding for each direction and loco holding at each end. At entry-level, I would recommend using the ex-GWR/BR locos available ready-to-run and if you are looking for added operational value, why not fictitiously continue running passenger services into BR steam days?

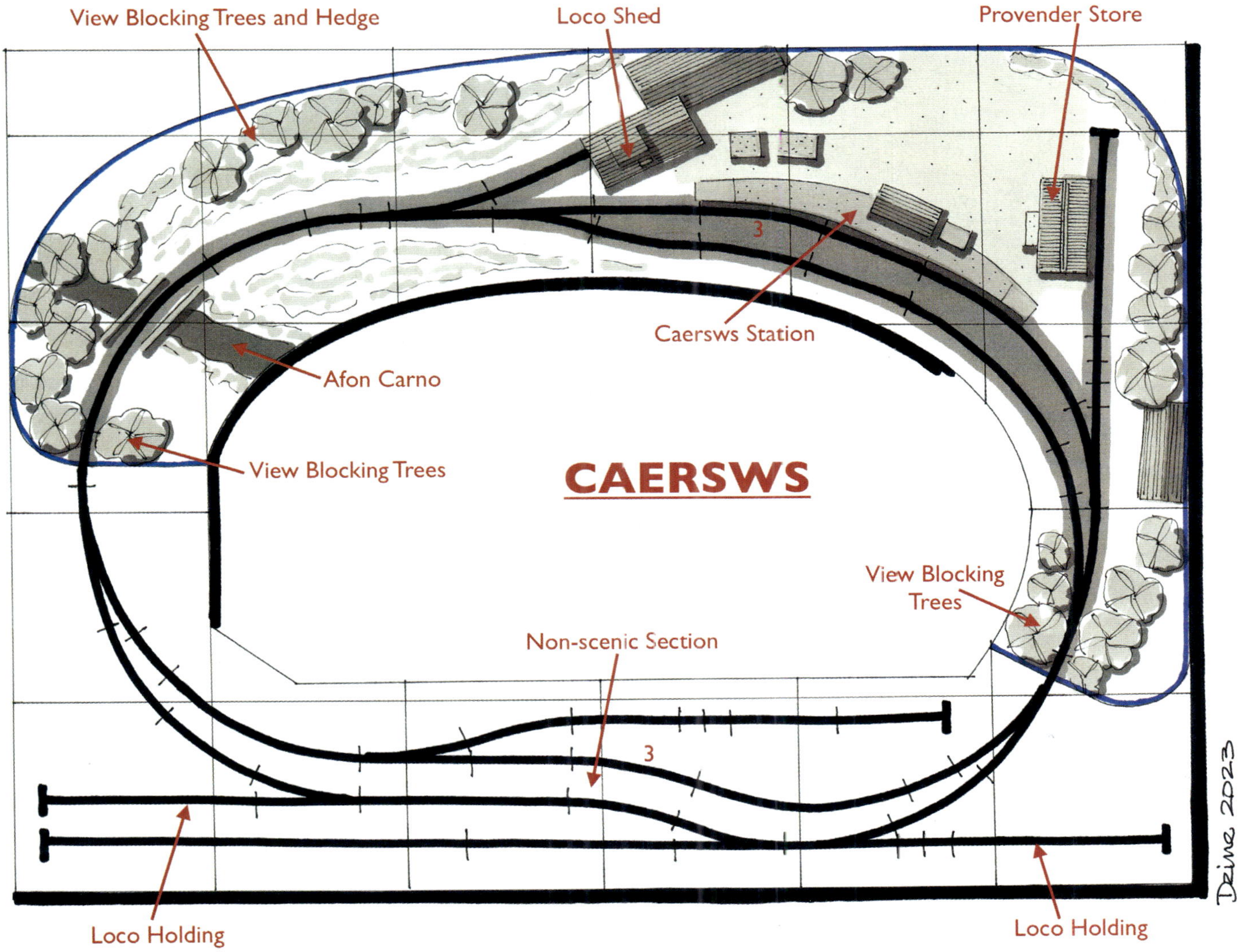

Snowdon Mountain Railway

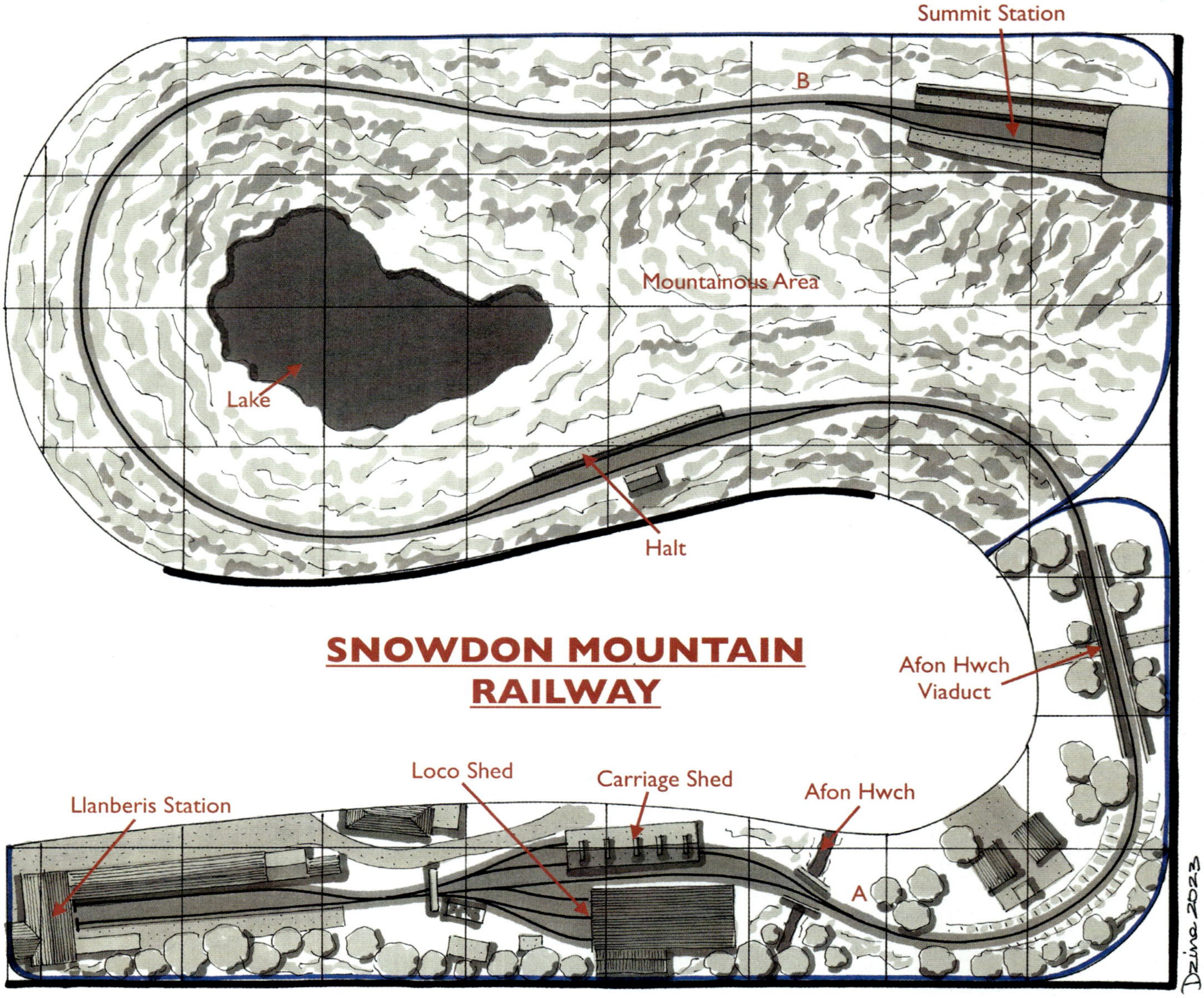

History and description at a glance

This 8ft 4in by 7ft 'S' shaped plan is for 009 or HOn. It rises continually from beyond the main line point, to the left of the loco shed, to just before the point at Clogwyn, then easing in grade through Clogwyn station and rising up again to just before the point giving access to Summit station. If you consider the grade between Llanberis and Clogwyn as a 6ft run and that between Clogwyn and Summit as an 8ft run, then with DCC Concepts that is going to be a total rise of a little over 16in, whereas with Ferro Trains it could be as much as 3ft 6in (see the More Modelling inspiration section over the page). I think even for the prototype, that is a little steep so it may be worth easing it out a bit. My take on this would be to make a full size mock-up to find out what looks right, which is admittedly time consuming but worth the effort. A final word on considering the scenic treatment. I think the terrain between Clogwyn and the semi-circular curve, to the baseboard edge, should fall away. Between Clogwyn and Summit, it should rise up with a slight dip for the lake.

The line was opened on April 6, 1896, as a 2ft 7½in gauge single track measuring 7.53km in length and with three passing loops. The average gradient is 1:7.8 with the steepest section at 1:5.5, the line rising 3,493ft overall (that is over 45ft high in

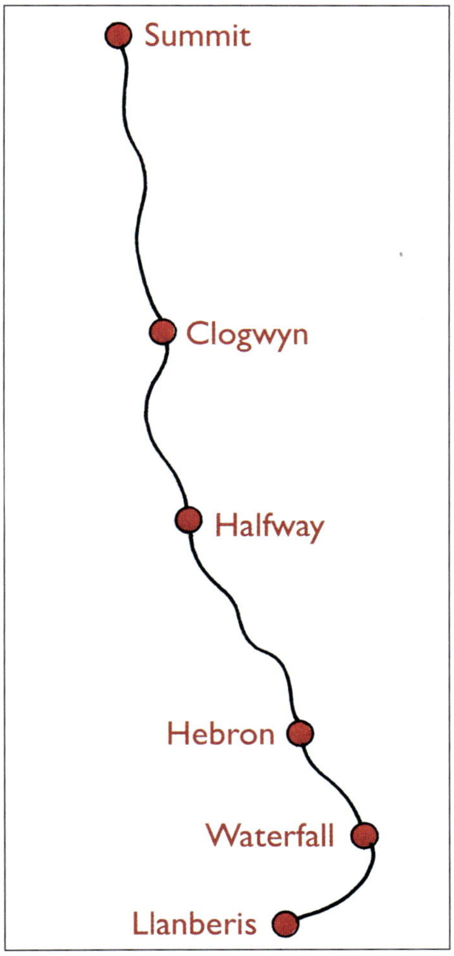

OO gauge) and traversed at a speed of approximately 5mph. It uses a rack and pinion Abt system developed by Dr. Roman Abt, who was a Swiss railway engineer. This consists of two offset racks that match two cogs on each axle of every locomotive, the system also acting as a brake.

It is possible to run two trains at a time as all platforms and stations have sufficient capacity. Llanberis has arrival and departure platforms while, at the Summit, trains tend to alternate between two tracks. The diesel locos usually lead up the mountain whereas steam locos push. Water tanks are available at Llanberis, Halfway and Clogwyn, and coal at Llanberis. Diesel requirements are less and therefore faster to turn round at Llanberis.

Period postcards are a great way to find out how something appeared in the past, rather than focussing too much on current operation, helpful as that is. As a result, I have included several here to aid that modelling process, including this near the summit. Note the protective boards either side of the rack and the extended sleepers.

Location by location

LEFT: **Llanberis station** has its original wooden buildings with later added canopies. There is a loco shed, coaling stage, diesel and water tanks, and a lifting gantry nearby. Afon Hwch Viaduct, on a 1:8.5 grade, is situated a short distance outside of the station.

Waterfall station opened on April 6, 1896, and closed in September 1923, being built to enable tourists to access the nearby Ceunant Mawr waterfall. The building is a rendered and timber construction and is used by engineers, but the single platform has been demolished. The gradient through the station is 1:20 and there was a siding here until 1905. During the later part of 2016, two new platforms were built, one either side of the line. After leaving the station, you pass the tree line and cross over the Afon Hwch again, on a 50ft arched bridge.

ABOVE: **This brick-lined, stone-arched bridge over Llanberis Path is situated on the section of track between Waterfall and Hebron stations.**

ABOVE: **Looking back towards Llanberis, and still at the lower levels, is this steam-operated train, pushing its way to the summit.**

Hebron Station, previously named Chapel station, is an intermediate passing place with watering facilities and a disused building. The latter is slate-roofed with rendered brick walls and a footprint of 23 metres by 4.5 metres. There was a short goods siding here to 1920 or so, and a footpath that leads to Halfway House café.

Halfway Station. There is a rock cutting just before Halfway and this is particularly useful for modelling purposes to hide a line going onto a non-scenic section. Locos refill with water here and there is a nearby café. There is a single platform and hipped-roof station building with rendered walls. The original wooden blockman's shelter burned down in 1910.

Rocky Valley Halt opened in 1974 and is a very basic concrete-topped platform, sheltered by a rocky outcrop. Trains sometimes terminate here if weather conditions demand.

ABOVE: **Clogwyn** **is an intermediate station situated on an exposed ridge overlooking Llanberis Pass 2,000ft below. Trains also terminate here in really bad weather. It now has a slabbed platform, gable-ended building with felted roof and twin solar panels, and water cranes at both ends of the station. Beyond Clogwyn, the terrain becomes really mountainous. Note a steep change in the gradient beyond the station, semaphore signalling, boarded access to this side of the loco cab and curtained coach apertures. You cannot say windows because they are non-existent!**

ABOVE LEFT AND ABOVE RIGHT: **Summit station is below the actual mountain summit. The first non-railway related buildings were erected in 1838 and then for railway use in 1896. A new station opened in 1936 with the first floor brought into use a year later. This was designed by Sir Clough Williams-Ellis, of Port Merrion fame, although due to its condition was demolished 2006. During the time of building works, trains terminated at Clogwyn. The current, Hafod Eryri, building was opened in 2009 and while there were many complaints about its predecessor, from my point of view, this latest replacement, in the shape of an upturned ship, leaves much to be desired.**

There are six small bridges on the line and signalling, with ground frames, was provided by the Railway Signal Co., Liverpool, and was still in use in the 1920s.

Stock

LEFT: There have been up to eight 0-4-2T steam locos, with their boilers mounted at a nine degree angle so the tubes are always full of water. Locos always ascend chimney first and are not coupled to a coach, which is always pushed up the mountain and kept in position by gravity. Since 1986, there have been five diesels and three diesel multiple units, although the latter are no longer used. One of the more interesting services, seen here, is a staff/provisions and works train, which often runs in the early morning.

More modelling inspiration

Austrian company Ferro Train produces an HOn narrow gauge rack and pinion system together with fully operational stock and while the latter is clearly of European outline, I am sure it is suitable for a makeover. The promotional material suggests a maximum 1:4 incline and curves down to 300mm radius. While impressive, such statistics need to be taken as being an indication that could change quite dramatically according to application, for example the load and gradient on a curve. Plain track comes in a one metre kit consisting of sleepers and centralised rack, separate running rails and fishplates. When bending a curve, the rack becomes the defining radius with one running rail cut shorter to suit the inner, reduced curve and the other longer to suit the outer, increasing curve. In addition, there are other complete ready-made items, including points (353mm curve radius) and a level crossing. If you are into scratchbuilding or adapting rolling stock, Fleischmann make rack and pinion track in HO and N.

Ever one to be on the lookout for an entry-level solution, I came up with the idea of using DCC Concepts' Power Base system and having the rack (possibly from cable ties or similar, depending on gauge) as a dummy feature. Wanting to put the process to the test, I spoke to DCC Concepts about my idea, but they were reluctant to commit due to many variables. I get that as it is to do with magnet position, depth, weight of loco, and so on. What they were able to say was that in a real test they managed to get a Hornby Pug to pull two or three wagons up a 1:10 gradient. To me, that is pretty impressive, but it is all about the compromise.

Whatever scale/gauge you choose and whether operational or purely cosmetic rack and pinion, the accompanying plan for HOn or 009 can be used, depending on available resources. This layout occupies a space of 7ft 6in by 4ft and comprises two scenes divided by a double sided backscene. For ease, the Llanberis station section is on the level, as is the non-scenic turntable. The track rises from entering the scenic mountainous section up to the toe of the point at Summit station. This is about a 3ft run, rising about 3½ inches with the DCC Concepts method, while with the Ferro train it could be as much as a 10 inch rise. Note the baseboard at the front of the mountain section will be considerably lower than the turntable, which is there to keep trains moving in the correct direction when transferring from one side of the baseboard to the other. Use a larger diameter turntable and reduce the summit section to fit if modelling the multiple unit period.

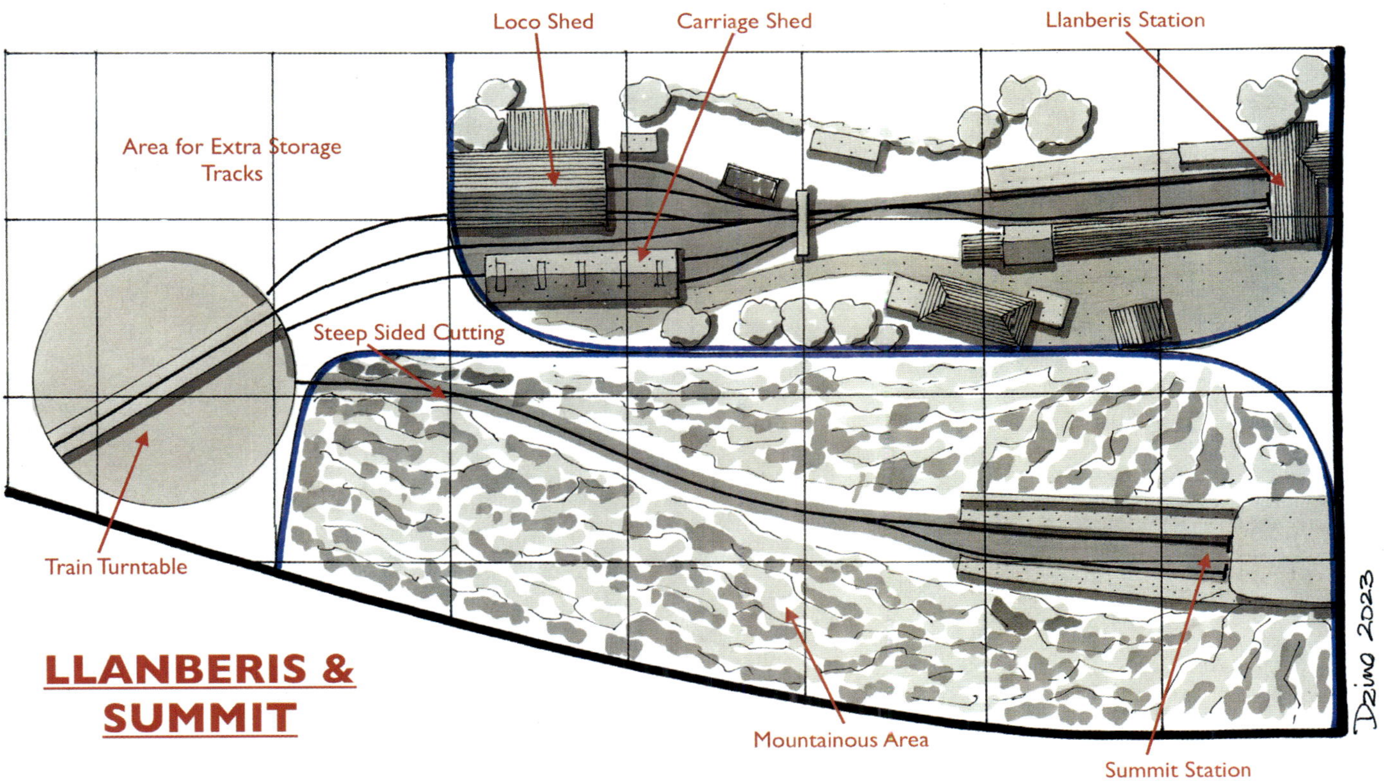

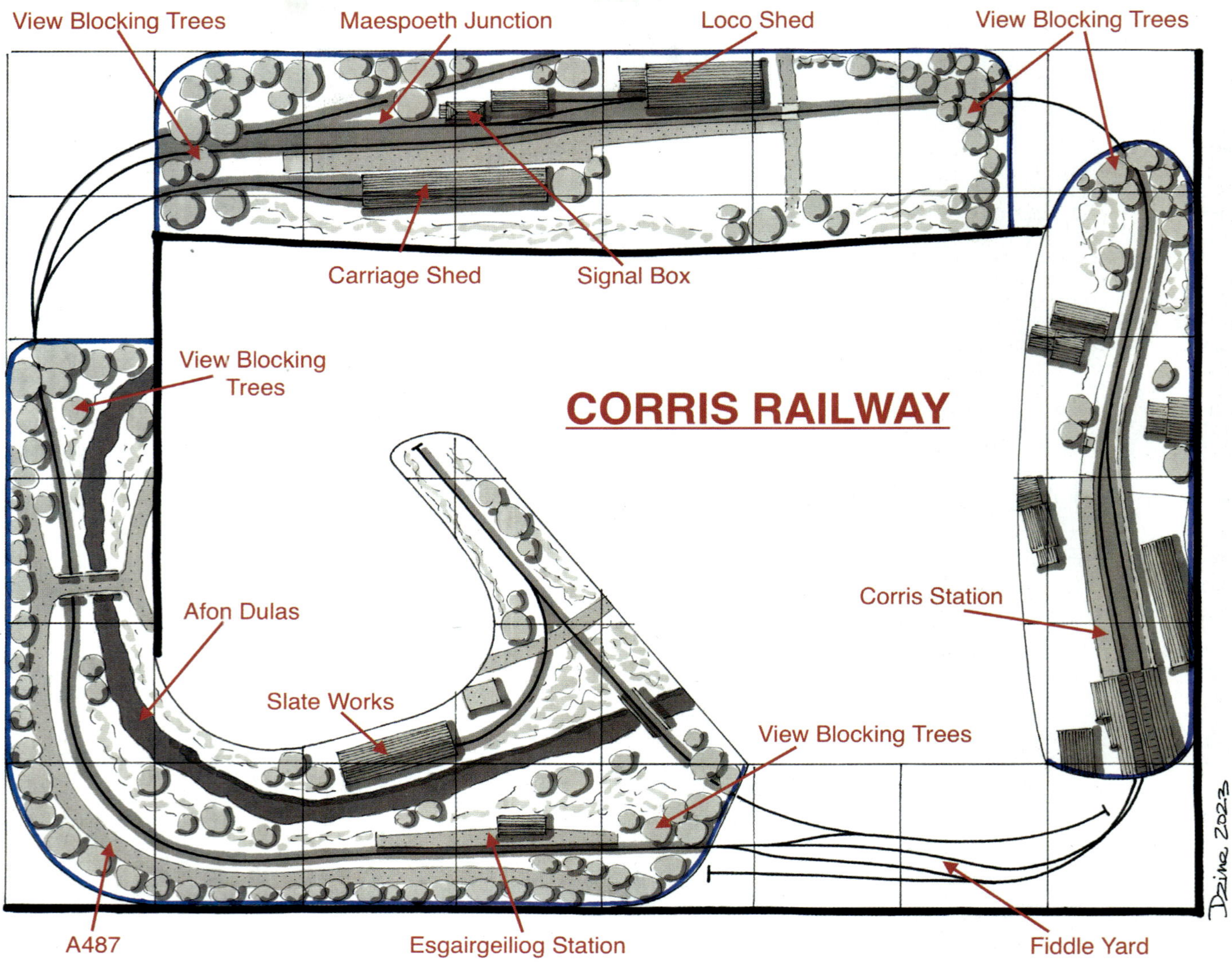

Corris Railway

History and description at a glance

There are two broad options for modelling the railway, the first being to go historical with the late 1800s/early 1900s period. I am told by one of the volunteers that, if you know where to look, there is quite a bit of the trackbed and architectural features relating to the original route that can still be traced. Alternately, you can replicate the present day scene or, if you are really flexible, possibly both! This 8ft by 6ft layout in 009 illustrates that point, in that I have shown Corris station and its hoped for replica building with overall roof. With a replacement building, it could be the present day terminus or an olden days through station feeding into a non-scenic fiddle yard beyond. At the opposite end, you could build on to Maespoeth and the current railhead in a 'L' shaped format. Further along, you can add the most scenic section along the Afon Dulas, and then on to Esgairgeiliog station. This could either be a preserved interpretation or with the slate works, this serving two nearby quarries and closed in the late 1920s. It kicks back onto a small peninsula baseboard, which is easily omitted if not of your chosen time period. I have added an operational link to the fiddle yard for both running in on the entire oval, or as if continuing to Machynlleth for period modellers.

The Corris Railway started life as a horse and gravity tramway from Corris Uchaf and Aberllefenni quarries, transporting slate to the River Dovey from 1859 to 1879, when Hughes steam locos were introduced. By the 1860s, slate was sent to interchange sidings at Machynlleth, and the passenger service commenced, after a fashion, in wagons during the 1870s. The line was purchased by Imperial Tramways Ltd, which introduced three steam locos and ten carriages but a dispute with the quarry owners meant the service was suspended in 1883. The railway prospered for the rest of the century, but this was followed by a decline in demand for slate, which was made worse by competition from road transportation.

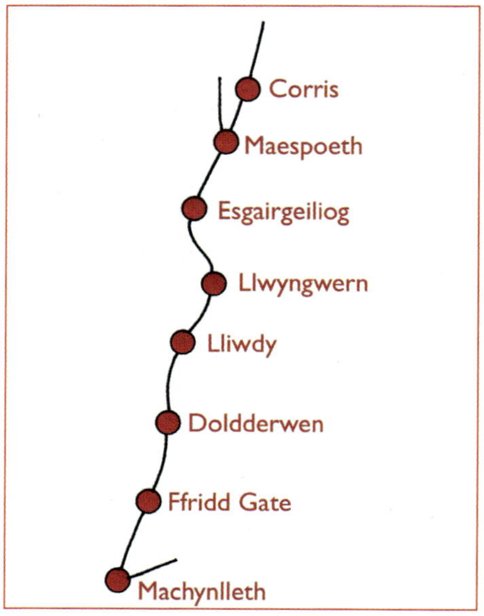

The 2ft 3in gauge line was purchased in 1930 by the GWR with passenger services then withdrawn, although goods traffic continued until final closure by BR in 1948. At this time, the surviving stock and locos were transferred to the Talyllyn Railway. In 1966, a preservation society was formed with the line along the Dulas Valley from Corris to Maespoeth opening in 2002. The first new steam loco arrived during 2005, while there is a southerly extension in progress, initially to Pont Evans and then onto the already restored station at Esgairgeiliog.

The current line has squeezed back into a narrow location at Corris, gently snaking its way, first close to Maes-y-Llan and then the A487 at Maespoeth Junction. From here, much of the line, and planned extension, will be in a very small gap between the A487 and Afon Dulas. Please note I have only included those locations with a passenger service.

Location by location

ABOVE: **Corris** at the moment is a basic station with a solitary platform, two-lever ground frame and run-round loop using a traverser built by Statfold Engineering due to the lack of space. There are hopes to erect a station building and canopy along the lines of the original in close proximity to the old stables, now used as a museum for the railway. The original station had stables, a parcels office, carriage shed and signal box until the mid-1940s.

ABOVE AND OPPOSITE: **Maespoeth Junction** has a lengthy, staggered platform in two parts, the original Corris engine shed, and replacement carriage shed and a signal box. The engine shed, used by the Forestry Commission in the 1950s, was built to hold three Hughes locomotives. It also features a small workshop, erected in 1878, and stables for horses working the upper Corris branch to Abercorris. The whole site was purchased by the Corris Railway Society in 2002.

NOT PICTURED: **Esgairgeiliog**, near the Dulas River, is a preserved station without track and consists of a slate-built shelter. There was a junction with a ground frame serving the Era Quarry Tramway and a nearby slate works.

Llwyngwern also had a junction, with headshunt and ground frame, for the horse-drawn tramway to the nearby Llwyngwern Quarry. The station buildings still survive and were built from slate with a corrugated metal platform store.

Lliwdy was an unofficial stopping place.

Doldderwen was an unofficial stopping place with a nearby level crossing.

Tan-y-Coed is a proposed station for the preserved railway, serving a Natural Resources picnic site.

Ffridd Gate has a level crossing over the B4404 and a ground frame. The building survives as a private residence.

Machynlleth consisted of multiple loops and interchanges at both ends of the standard gauge yard, together with a loco shed, which was removed in 1938. Machynlleth station building is a substantial structure and still remains in situ.

Original locos

No.1 - Hughes Locomotive and Tramway Engineering Works, rebuilt as a 0-4-0ST in 1895.

No.2 - Hughes Locomotive and Tramway Engineering Works, rebuilt as a 0-4-0ST in 1898.

No.3 - Hughes Locomotive and Tramway Engineering Works, rebuilt as a 0-4-0ST in 1900.

No.4 - Hughes Kerr Stuart and Co., a 0-4-2ST from 1921.

Talyllyn Railway

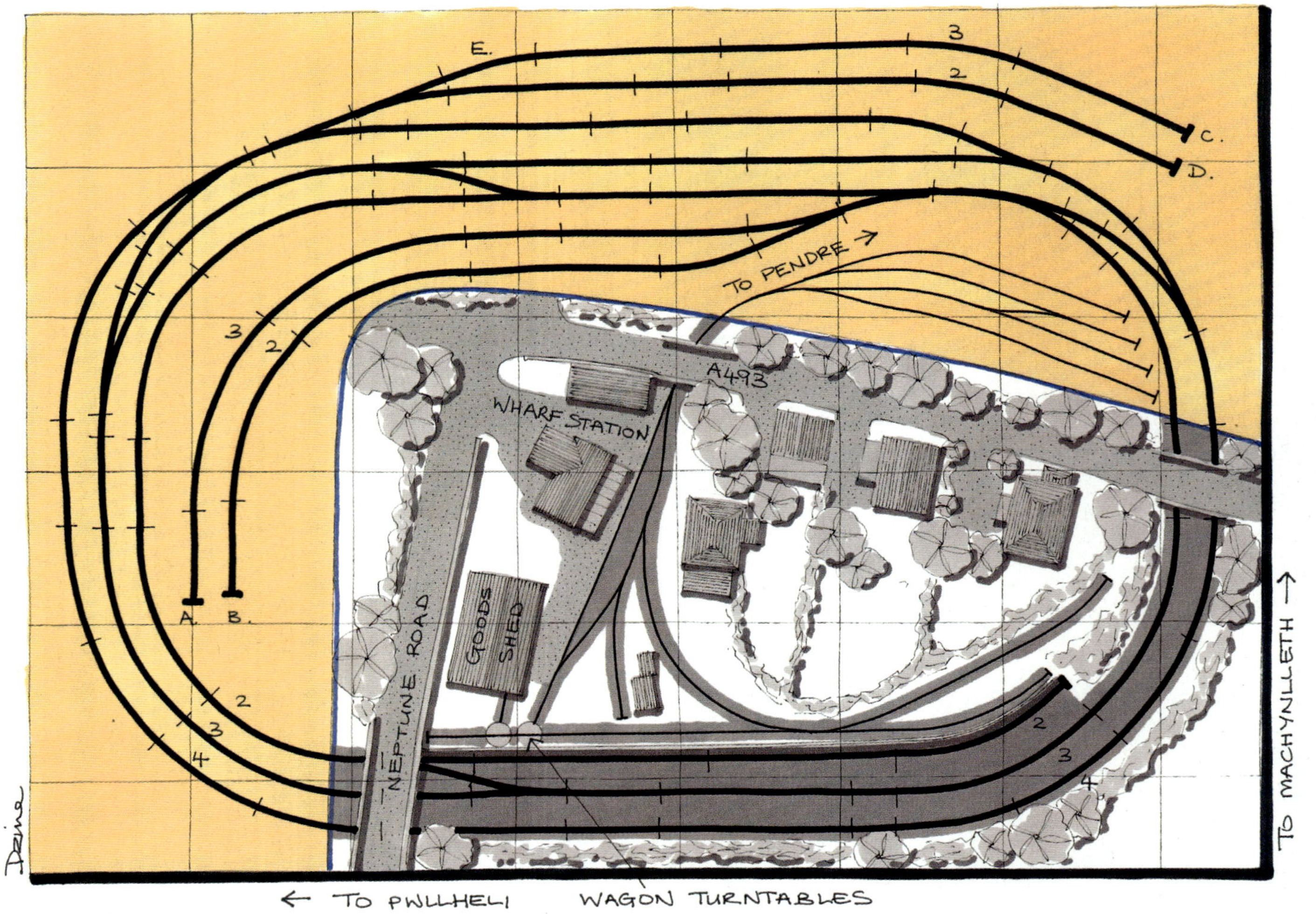

History and description at a glance

Functionally, I am really pleased with the accompanying 7ft 6in by 5ft 6in OO and OO9 gauge design, but it does break one of my cardinal rules in that more than 50 percent of the baseboard is non-scenic. Part of the issue is there are two reasonably complex track arrangements in close proximity and, of course, two fiddle yards. That said, there is substantial scenic depth and the relationship between both gauges is very similar to the real place.

This 2ft 3in gauge, 7.25 miles long railway opened in 1866 to carry slate from Bryn Eglwys Quarry, beyond Nant Gwernol, to the wharves at Tywyn, where it meets the ex-Cambrian Railway. It was the first railway in the world to be preserved by volunteers.

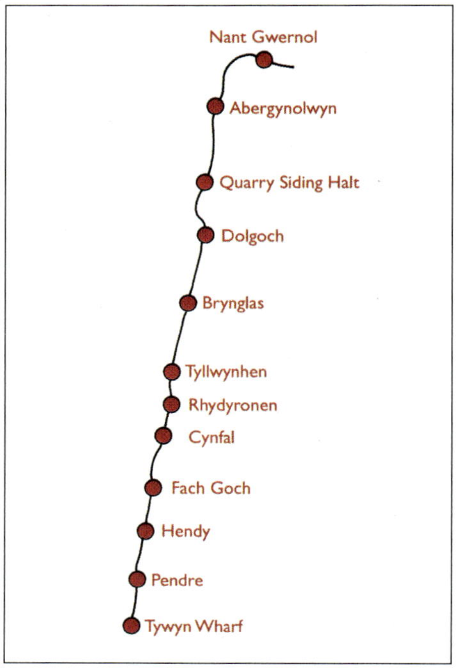

Location by location

Nant Gwernol re-opened as part of the preserved railway in 1976. It was originally a mineral line serving Bryn Eglwys Quarry. The current station is built on the site of sidings at the foot of Alltwyllt Incline, which served the quarry.

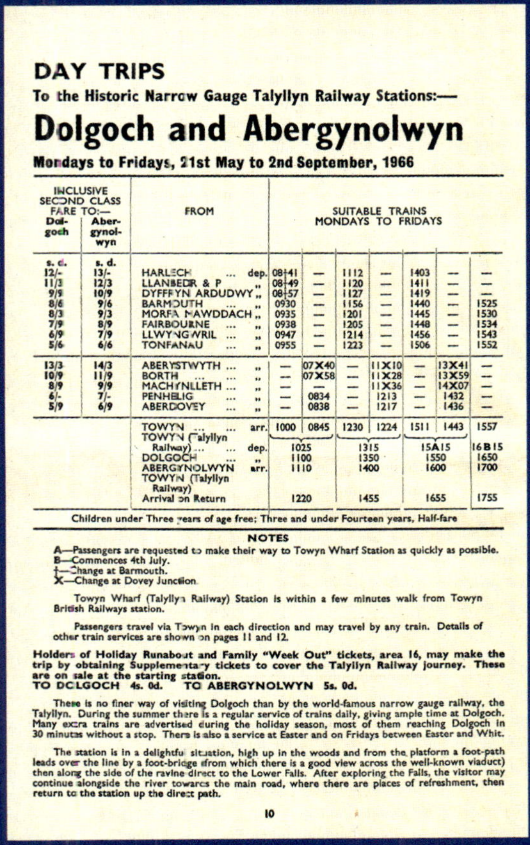

DAY TRIPS

To the Historic Narrow Gauge Talyllyn Railway Stations:—

Dolgoch and Abergynolwyn

Mondays to Fridays, 21st May to 2nd September, 1966

INCLUSIVE SECOND CLASS FARE TO:— Dolgoch	Abergynolwyn	FROM		SUITABLE TRAINS MONDAYS TO FRIDAYS						
s. d.	s. d.									
12/-	13/-	HARLECH ...	dep.	08†41	—	1112	—	1403	—	—
11/3	12/3	LLANBEDR & P	,,	08†49	—	1120	—	1411	—	—
9/9	10/9	DYFFRYN ARDUDWY	,,	08†57	—	1127	—	1419	—	—
8/6	9/6	BARMOUTH ...	,,	0930	—	1156	—	1440	—	1525
8/3	9/3	MORFA MAWDDACH	,,	0935	—	1201	—	1445	—	1530
7/9	8/9	FAIRBOURNE ...	,,	0938	—	1205	—	1448	—	1534
6/9	7/9	LLWYNGWRIL ...	,,	0947	—	1214	—	1456	—	1543
5/6	6/6	TONFANAU ...	,,	0955	—	1223	—	1506	—	1552
13/3	14/3	ABERYSTWYTH ...	,,	—	07X40	—	11X10	—	13X41	—
10/9	11/9	BORTH	,,	—	07X58	—	11X28	—	13X59	—
8/9	9/9	MACHYNLLETH ...	,,	—	—	—	11X36	—	14X07	—
6/-	7/-	PENHELIG ...	,,	—	0834	—	1213	—	1432	—
5/9	6/9	ABERDOVEY ...	,,	—	0838	—	1217	—	1436	—
		TOWYN	arr.	1000	0845	1230	1224	1511	1443	1557
		TOWYN (Talyllyn Railway)	dep.	1025		1315		15A15		16B15
		DOLGOCH ...	,,	1100		1350		1550		1650
		ABERGYNOLWYN	arr.	1110		1400		1600		1700
		TOWYN (Talyllyn Railway) Arrival on Return		1220		1455		1655		1755

Children under Three years of age free; Three and under Fourteen years, Half-fare

NOTES

A—Passengers are requested to make their way to Towyn Wharf Station as quickly as possible.
B—Commences 4th July.
†—Change at Barmouth.
X—Change at Dovey Junction.

Towyn Wharf (Talyllyn Railway) Station is within a few minutes walk from Towyn British Railways station.

Passengers travel via Towyn in each direction and may travel by any train. Details of other train services are shown on pages 11 and 12.

Holders of Holiday Runabout and Family "Week Out" tickets, area 16, may make the trip by obtaining Supplementary tickets to cover the Talyllyn Railway journey. These are on sale at the starting station.
TO DOLGOCH 4s. 0d. TO ABERGYNOLWYN 5s. 0d.

There is no finer way of visiting Dolgoch than by the world-famous narrow gauge railway, the Talyllyn. During the summer there is a regular service of trains daily, giving ample time at Dolgoch. Many extra trains are advertised during the holiday season, most of them reaching Dolgoch in 30 minutes without a stop. There is also a service at Easter and on Fridays between Easter and Whit.

The station is in a delightful situation, high up in the woods and from the platform a foot-path leads over the line by a foot-bridge (from which there is a good view across the well-known viaduct) then along the side of the ravine direct to the Lower Falls. After exploring the Falls, the visitor may continue alongside the river towards the main road, where there are places of refreshment, then return to the station up the direct path.

10

Abergynolwyn is the original terminus and is situated on a ledge, its 620ft long platform being capable of serving two trains. There was a single siding to the west end of the station, which was used to load pit props during the Second World War before it closed in the early 1950s. The current slate station building dates from 1969 and replaces an earlier timber version.

Quarry Siding was previously known as Tanycoed and served a nearby shale quarry. There is a passing loop with five lever ground frame and a carriage shed.

Dolgoch Viaduct dates from 1865 and is constructed from red brick with stone detailing. There are three segmented spans on two slightly tapering piers and a metal fence and refuges on the parapet walls. There are rock cuttings either side of the viaduct which stands approximately 52ft high.

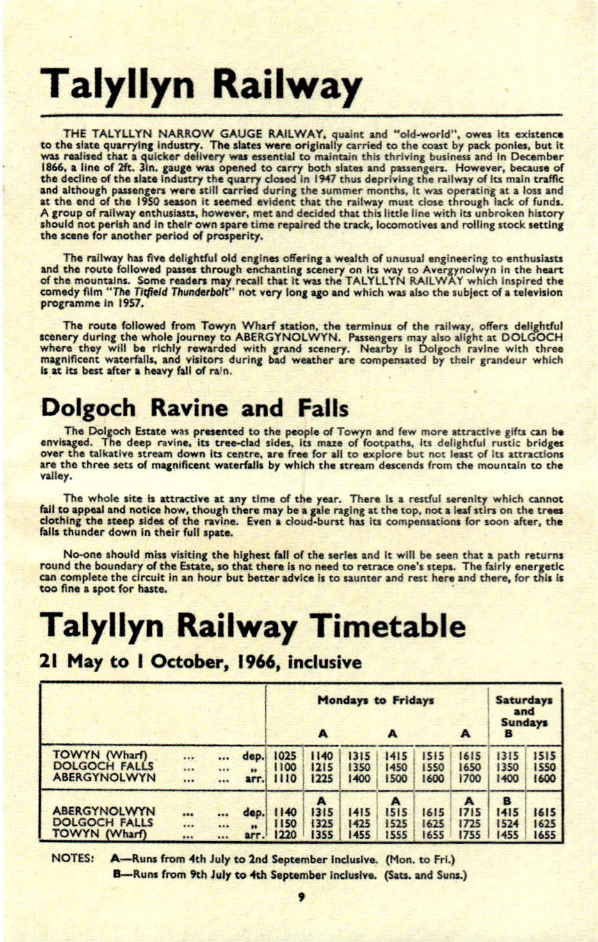

Talyllyn Railway

THE TALYLLYN NARROW GAUGE RAILWAY, quaint and "old-world", owes its existence to the slate quarrying industry. The slates were originally carried to the coast by pack ponies, but it was realised that a quicker delivery was essential to maintain this thriving business and in December 1866, a line of 2ft. 3in. gauge was opened to carry both slates and passengers. However, because of the decline of the slate industry the quarry closed in 1947 thus depriving the railway of its main traffic and although passengers were still carried during the summer months, it was operating at a loss and at the end of the 1950 season it seemed evident that the railway must close through lack of funds. A group of railway enthusiasts, however, met and decided that this little line with its unbroken history should not perish and in their own spare time repaired the track, locomotives and rolling stock setting the scene for another period of prosperity.

The railway has five delightful old engines offering a wealth of unusual engineering to enthusiasts and the route followed passes through enchanting scenery on its way to Avergynolwyn in the heart of the mountains. Some readers may recall that it was the TALYLLYN RAILWAY which inspired the comedy film "*The Titfield Thunderbolt*" not very long ago and which was also the subject of a television programme in 1957.

The route followed from Towyn Wharf station, the terminus of the railway, offers delightful scenery during the whole journey to ABERGYNOLWYN. Passengers may also alight at DOLGOCH where they will be richly rewarded with grand scenery. Nearby is Dolgoch ravine with three magnificent waterfalls, and visitors during bad weather are compensated by their grandeur which is at its best after a heavy fall of rain.

Dolgoch Ravine and Falls

The Dolgoch Estate was presented to the people of Towyn and few more attractive gifts can be envisaged. The deep ravine, its tree-clad sides, its maze of footpaths, its delightful rustic bridges over the talkative stream down its centre, are free for all to explore but not least of its attractions are the three sets of magnificent waterfalls by which the stream descends from the mountain to the valley.

The whole site is attractive at any time of the year. There is a restful serenity which cannot fail to appeal and notice how, though there may be a gale raging at the top, not a leaf stirs on the trees clothing the steep sides of the ravine. Even a cloud-burst has its compensations for soon after, the falls thunder down in their full spate.

No-one should miss visiting the highest fall of the series and it will be seen that a path returns round the boundary of the Estate, so that there is no need to retrace one's steps. The fairly energetic can complete the circuit in an hour but better advice is to saunter and rest here and there, for this is too fine a spot for haste.

Talyllyn Railway Timetable

21 May to 1 October, 1966, inclusive

		Mondays to Fridays						Saturdays and Sundays	
			A		A		A	B	
TOWYN (Wharf)	dep.	1025	1140	1315	1415	1515	1615	1315	1515
DOLGOCH FALLS	,,	1100	1215	1350	1450	1550	1650	1350	1550
ABERGYNOLWYN	arr.	1110	1225	1400	1500	1600	1700	1400	1600
			A		A		A	B	
ABERGYNOLWYN	dep.	1140	1315	1415	1515	1615	1715	1415	1615
DOLGOCH FALLS	,,	1150	1325	1425	1525	1625	1725	1524	1625
TOWYN (Wharf)	arr.	1220	1355	1455	1555	1655	1755	1455	1655

NOTES: A—Runs from 4th July to 2nd September inclusive. (Mon. to Fri.)
B—Runs from 9th July to 4th September inclusive. (Sats. and Suns.)

9

ABOVE: **Dolgoch** was opened by 1867 and has a station building built from slate blocks, along with a slightly curving platform covered with slate chippings and edged with slate slabs. The platform was extended, in both directions in 1961 and now has a tarmac surface. There are three water towers, two at the east end and one at the west. It is thought that a siding was provided to a nearby slate quarry at Dolgoch, which closed in 1884. There is access to the nearby falls and a footbridge was added to improve the route in 1958. The delightful model, one of the best I have seen, is part of a larger and ever expanding 009 building range from Matt at msmodelschesterfield@gmail.com. His station shelter at Dolgoch includes masses of detail and outstanding slate work.

ABOVE LEFT, ABOVE RIGHT AND OPPOSITE TOP LEFT & RIGHT : **Brynglas** serves the village of Pandy and has a slate shelter. The platform is covered slate chippings and edged with slate slabs of various sizes; it was extended in the 1990s. During 1953, the siding was converted into a passing loop and a further siding added in 1975 for wagon storage. A six-lever ground frame, by the level crossing, was exposed to the elements until the 1960s but is now enclosed, as you can see in the accompanying photo. Slate was transported from Cwm-Pandy Quarry, which closed around 1880. There is a level crossing at the northern end too and a brick arch bridge over the Afon Cwm-Pandy. Also from Matt at msmodelschesterfield@gmail.com is Brynglas station shelter, which is again finely modelled. Note that both of Matt's station buildings have been given a light spray of grey primer.

Tyllwynhen is a request stop and consists of a very basic arrangement with no platform. There are a few boards for a farm track crossing and only a small rough ground area on which to alight.

ABOVE LEFT, ABOVE RIGHT AND RIGHT: **Rhydyronen** was opened in February 1867 and is also a request stop. It was the first intermediate station with a station building made from slate and a platform of slate chippings edged with slate slabs, this being extended in 1979 and again in the 1990s. There was a passing loop for a local quarry and mines nearby, while a siding was used for refuge until 1951, being removed three years later and then reinstated as an engineers' loop in 1956/57, it often housed locos and trolleys. The west end loop point was removed in 1971 and the rest in August 1977.

Cynfal is a request stop and has a very short platform made from slabs on top of aerated blocks. A slate with red brick arch and buttresses bridge is immediately adjacent.

Fach Goch request stop is situated near a grassy area and farm track, there was a siding here between 1971 and 1982 for depositing waste material.

Hendy request stop has a small slate chipped area at ground level and a wooden seat.

Pendre opened in February 1867 with a single-storey timber station building that dates from November 1866. There are loco and carriage sheds here at the heart of the railway. The slate-built loco shed originally had a cottage attached for an engine driver and was later used as a crossing keeper's house. It then became part of the shed in 1968, with a plaque recognising the change of use. There are several carriage sheds, one in timber and brick, with the others from what looks like corrugated asbestos sheet. There is a 15-lever ground frame cabin added in front of the west carriage shed and a level crossing, which was widened in 1983, at the station end. The loop here now dates from 1952, prior to that trains had to be propelled to the Wharf station.

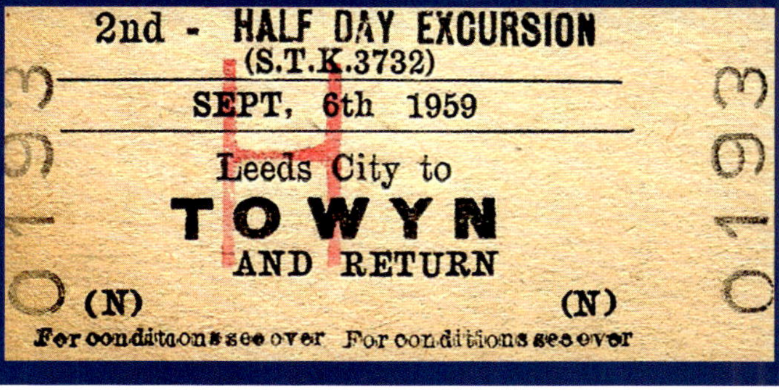

Tywyn Wharf was originally named King's station, although it was not a passenger station but a place for the transhipment of slate onto the Cambrian Railway. At this time, passenger services started from Pendre. Passenger trains commenced from here in the early 1900s and the station was renamed Towyn Wharf with a Victorian-style brick-built station and cast iron canopy. A loop was added in 1951/52 after preservation and the site has sidings, a coaling stage, and a water tower.

More modelling inspiration

If your priority is in operation, Wharf station and the entire site at Pendre offer the two most intensively active parts of the railway. In 009, it is possible to represent both of these in a space of 6ft by 4ft in an end-to-end layout in oval format. There is, from my point of view, one required compromise in that, whichever way you orientate the design, either Wharf station or the longest run of sheds at Pendre end up being on the outer edge of the baseboard and therefore view block quite a section of track. Of the two, my preference is to have them as shown on the plan and reduce the length of the buildings at Wharf station.

By contrast, if a rural scene is your priority, then Rhydyronen and Brynglas both have or had passing loops and a siding and are set in beautiful locations. Perfect if you are looking for a basic oval and one station, or as second fiddle to the Wharf or Pendre in a 'L' or 'U' shaped plan. If you want wow factor then Dolgoch station and the nearby viaduct is the one, but model it back in the day when there was much less vegetation.

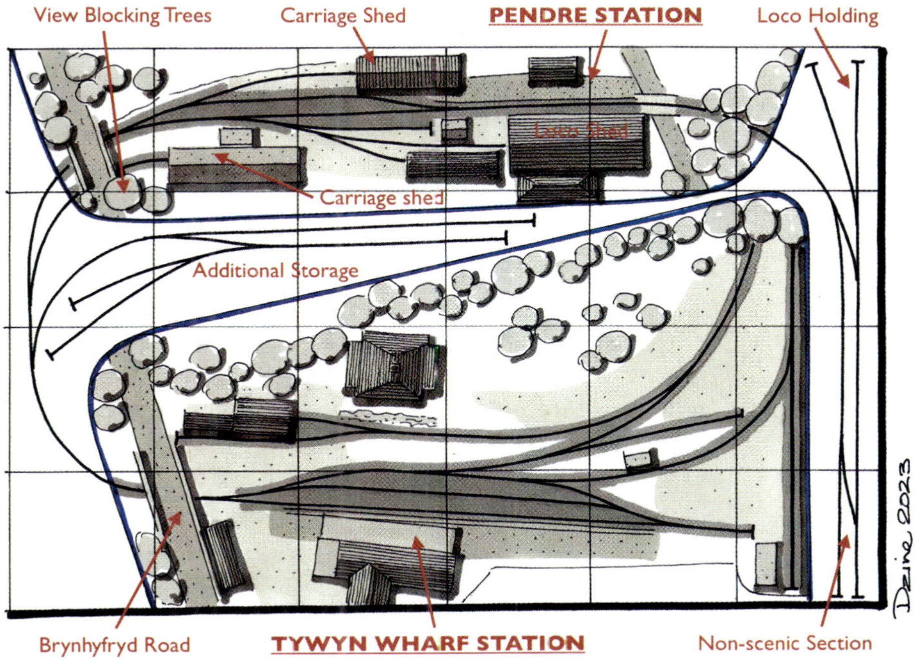

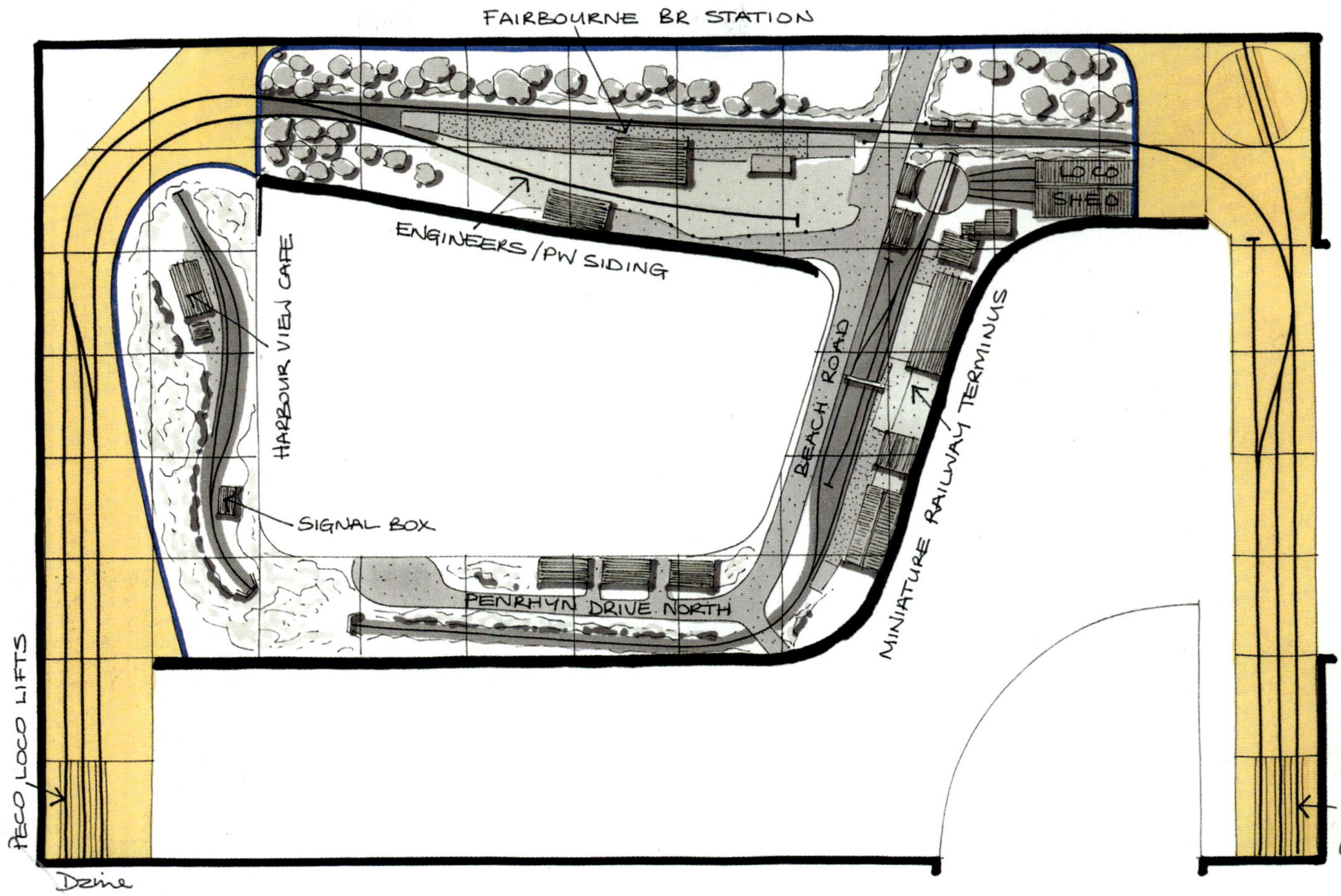

Fairbourne Miniature Railway

History and description at a glance

The line is approximately two miles long and during its life has terminated either at Penrhyn Point or, more recently, at Barmouth Ferry station, where you can board a ferry boat to Barmouth. The location is exposed and can be subjected to extreme weather events, but there are outstanding views of Cader Idris, Mawddach Estuary and Barmouth Bridge.

The original 2ft gauge line opened in 1895 as a horse drawn tramway, with a view to helping the construction and development of Fairbourne as a holiday resort. This never came to fruition but as a hint of things to come, the tramway started to carry passengers towards the end of its life. In 1916, it was bought by Narrow Gauge Railways Ltd, then owners of the Ravensglass and Eskdale Railway, and was converted into 15 inch gauge.

By 1922, the railway was operated by Barmouth Motor Boat and Ferry Co, with Fairbourne Estate and Development Co taking over in 1925. The line closed in 1940 after operating with diesel traction only and went through a period of decline. Following the Second World War, it was re-opened in 1947 by the Fairbourne Railway Co.

Eventually, the Ellerton family bought the line in 1984 with the intention of converting it to 12¼in gauge. The last 15in gauge train ran on September 15, 1985, with all the stock departing thereafter. Re-gauging then started as well as adding new carriage and loco sheds and a tunnel, with re-opening coming in 1986. New steam locos were all half-sized replicas. The line was purchased in 1995 by Tony Atkinson and Roger Melton and became a charity, North Wales Coast Light Railway Ltd, in 2008.

ABOVE: **Although substantially compressed; BR in OO and the Fairbourne Miniature Railway in N, this is a combined design offering an instant way of modelling the prototypes together, even if there is a compromise on gauge (see comments overleaf). I am pleased that, in an area of 12ft by 8ft, many key components have been included and that the geographic orientation is correct for all four sides. That said, I have reduced and modified the trackplan around the loco shed area for a more entry-level arrangement, reduced the station run alongside Beach Road, and missed out all the intermediate halts. The main line BR operation could be represented as it is now, or throughout the BR steam and diesel periods.**

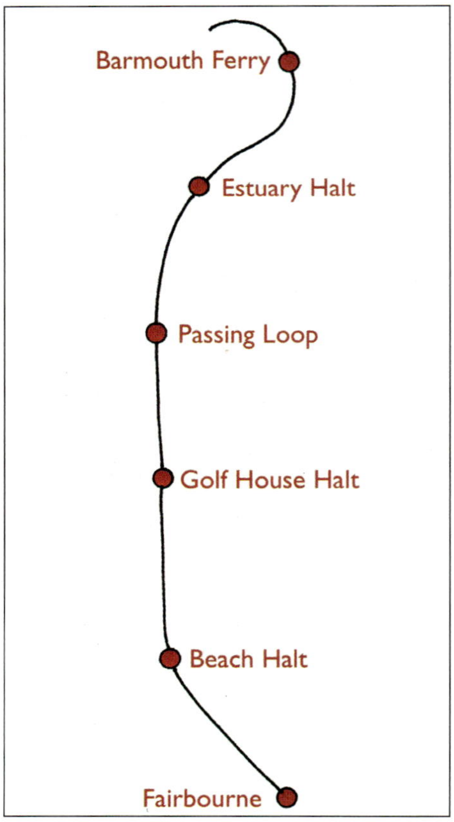

Location by location

ABOVE AND LEFT: **Return loop** was last used on July 27, 2013. Sections can still be seen half buried in the sand and are testimony to the extreme conditions, especially sand drifts from high winds, on the outer side of the peninsula.

ABOVE LEFT, ABOVE RIGHT AND LEFT: **Penrhyn Point/Barmouth Ferry station.** The original tramway terminus was at Penrhyn Point on the seaward side of the peninsula, near to where the disused return loop is now, whereas the much later Barmouth Ferry station, seen here, is on the sheltered eastern side.

ABOVE: **Jack Steele Tunnel** was built in 1987 from brick and rendered blockwork. There had been a second tunnel, but it was a wind trap and was subsequently removed.

ABOVE: **Estuary Halt** is a request stop with a ground level platform covered with crushed slate. It has a sign and is adjacent to Jack Steele Tunnel.

Passing Loop is a request stop, installed in 1951. The platform is made up of crushed slate with a concrete edge.

Golf House Halt is a request stop with a slightly raised tarmac-finished platform, seat, and sign.

Beach Halt, formerly Bathing Beach, is a request stop with a slightly raised platform, this being finished with crushed slate and concrete edging stones.

ABOVE LEFT AND ABOVE RIGHT: **Fairbourne station** is the main terminus, parallel to Beach Road and set at 90 degrees to the BR main line. It has carriage and loco sheds in a corner setting, served by a sharp curve and turntable respectively, as seen on the plan. The station is an amalgam of several materials; being mainly block/brickwork with timber and corrugated roofed buildings and tarmac platforms. In previous years, there has been a cosmetic signal box, near to where the ground frame is situated. Note the close proximity to the BR station and the contrasting landscape with a flat plain and steeply rising hills.